How to Get Started as a MANUFACTURERS' REPRESENTATIVE

How to
Get Started
as a
MANUFACTURERS'
REPRESENTATIVE

William H. Krause

A Division of
AMERICAN MANAGEMENT
ASSOCIATIONS

Library of Congress Cataloging in Publication Data

Krause, William H
  How to get started as a manufacturers' representative.
  Includes index.
  1. Manufacturers' agents. 2. Manufacturers' agents—
Case studies. I. Title.
HF5422.K72   670′.68′8   79–54840
ISBN 0–8144–5584–0

©1980 AMACOM
A division of American Management Associations, New York.

FIRST PRINTING

TO MY WIFE, JOYCE

PREFACE

A NOT-SO-QUIET revolution is taking place in the offices of sales managers of manufacturing plants all over the country. Having watched the cost of maintaining a company salesman soar to approximately $40,000 a year, sales executives are rushing to sign up manufacturers' representatives to sell their goods. These independent commissioned salesmen (known as reps, sales agents, or sales representatives) usually represent a group of companies (known as principals) that manufacture compatible—but not competitive—products in an exclusive territory. Their only income is derived from commissions paid to them on the sale of goods; thus they give their principals a stable *cost of sales*. In addition, having worked a given territory over a period of years, they provide the manufacturer ready access to the market, and they are already trained professional salesmen.

There is only one problem. There simply aren't enough established professional reps to meet the increasing demand. Sales managers complain of being turned down repeatedly by reps who are already representing firms making similar products.

So industry desperately needs an influx of new reps to sell the products of thousands of companies that are turning to this age-old style of selling. Unfortunately, the influx hasn't arrived yet. This is somewhat puzzling and frustrating to the manufacturers, but there is a good reason for it. Although many men and women, mostly in sales positions, would like to get out on their own and become manufacturers' representatives, they too are puzzled and frustrated because they don't know *how to begin*. There's no franchiser who, for a fee and a royalty, can show them how to enter the rep field, nor are there night schools that feature courses on how to get into the rep business.

This book was written to fill the information gap and is intended primarily for the person who wants his own sales agency but doesn't know how to begin. It will cut through the mystique surrounding the manufacturers' representative business and will explain the essential ingredients for entering this field where the rewards, in both income and independence, are great.

I'd like to acknowledge the assistance of six established reps whose stories are related in the beginning chapters of this book. These men described the ups and downs of their early days to me, and I would like to pass their experiences—experiences that will be invaluable to the novice—on to you.

Charlie Holmes of the Lakewood Bank and Trust Company in Dallas literally gave me a course in retirement operations. His knowledge added greatly to the book.

I appreciate the efforts of my son Scott, who skillfully and courageously edited my business prose when his real interest lies with the works of Keats and Shelley—and an occasional novel by John McDonald. Joyce, my wife and live-in typist, not only typed the manuscript but tactfully suggested certain modifications in the text that improved the contents considerably.

WILLIAM H. KRAUSE

CONTENTS

How to Get Started as a MANUFACTURERS' REPRESENTATIVE

1
THE INDEPENDENT MANUFACTURERS' REPRESENTATIVE
A Realistic View

IF YOU WANTED to go into your own business—open a shoe store, start a cleaning service, or try a fast-food operation—you could visit your local bookstore or library and find on the shelves good, authoritative books on how to begin any of these ventures. These books would contain helpful hints about location, capital requirements, inventory needs, advertising techniques, and just about everything else a new entrepreneur needs to know to maximize his possibilities of success.

You might also find one or two books that outline the techniques needed to run a successful manufacturers' representative agency. These books would help in the administration of a first-rate sales agency by providing advice on selling strategies, office layout, advertising techniques, and bookkeeping procedures. However, no book I've been able to find on this subject really tells you *how to get started*. And if you don't know how to get started, it matters little whether or not you're a good salesman or administrator; you'll never have the opportunity to put your skills to work.

There is, of course, a perfectly legitimate reason for the omission. No single formula will guarantee successful entry into the ranks of professional manufacturers' representatives. What has worked for one potential enterpreneur won't necessarily work for another. No two reps in business have identical success stories. Almost every successful rep can recall a critical point somewhere along the line that made his decision to strike out on his own a natural course of action. It may have been an unexpected inheritance of a few thousand dollars, or a disagreement with his superior at work, or even the loss of his job. Whatever the actual reason, it provided a powerful motivation, for the beginning rep is completely on his own. He has no regular paycheck, no one to turn to for advice, no fringe benefits, and very little security.

This book is designed to eliminate most of the uncertainties facing the novice in this intriguing profession. By reading every chapter carefully and applying the lessons to your own situation, you too can reap the benefits of your own sales agency and learn the techniques that will greatly enhance your chances for success.

Before we get to the real-life experiences that will aid you in charting your own course, let's take a hard look at the hurdles that stand in your way. By facing them directly and honestly, you can more easily prepare for the steps that will take you from beginner to professional. After you've reviewed the challenges facing the beginning rep, you'll be better able to accept and carry out the strict disciplines that will assure you a successful and enjoyable future as a manufacturers' representative.

The new rep faces a very real deadline: the day the money runs out. He knows—or should know—that he has just so many months to reach breakeven status, just so much time to make enough sales to become self-sufficient. To add to his uncertainty, he must typically wait 60 to 90 days, or longer, for commissions *after* the sale is made. Often an inability to recognize this critical lag time can be enough to put even a successful salesman out of business. He can't afford to miscalculate the actual deadline facing him. If he hasn't allowed for this lag time and later seeks financing to carry him over those few extra months, he'll find that bankers and other financial sources are less than enthusiastic about lending money to a newly self-employed businessman.

The delayed-commission-payment principle is a fact of life for the rep. Let's take, for example, a representative who sells metal components such as steel castings or metal stampings. To begin with, the potential customer must need a newly designed component for his company's product, whether it be refrigerators or automobiles. The parts now used in production are already being made by another supplier, and expensive tooling has previously been purchased by the customer in order to make these component parts. Thus a buyer is unlikely to switch suppliers and invest additional thousands of dollars in tooling to make the same parts. The beginning représentative must wait for a new or improved model of the customer's product that will need parts of a different design and require new tooling.

When that time arrives—which may be a month or a year away—the customer will send out blueprints of the new part to several potential suppliers, most of them proven producers of similar parts. If the new representative has made a good impression on the customer's buyer, his company may get an opportunity to quote on the new part in competition with the other companies.

In a few weeks the representative's company will submit a bid on the new parts. In order to qualify for an order, its price must be sufficiently attractive to gain the buyer's attention. The buyer may then conduct a survey of the manufacturing capabilities of the representative's firm and certify the company as an approved source for the buyer's company. Then, and only then, will the representative receive an order. This could be anywhere from two months to two years after he originally solicited the potential customer's business.

After an order is received, it can take from two to four months for the tooling to be completed. Samples of the new parts are made and sent to the customer for his scrutiny. If they are approved, the company receives the O.K. to proceed with production. In a few weeks parts are shipped, and the customer is billed for them. But he may take from 60 to 90 days to pay—an increasingly common practice in today's capital-short industrial world.

Some of the representative's firms may pay commissions in the month following shipment, but approximately 45 percent of all firms pay the representative the month after receipt of payment from the customer. If payment is not received, no commission is paid.

An extreme illustration of lag time between the original sales call by a representative and the ultimate receipt of commissions is provided by the automobile manufacturers, who plan for each year's models several years in advance. The same is true for many other manufacturers such as those making household appliances, motorized lawn equipment, or over-the-road construction vehicles. In the construction industry, the same built-in delay is part of the representative's nightmare. A new industrial building or high-rise condominium must first be designed by an architect, who will be wooed by representatives selling building materials to make sure he specifies their products on the blueprints. Again, the period beginning with the original sales call by the representative on the architect through the ordering of the material by the contractor to actual shipment of the representatives's product can take up to three years.

These examples are the extremes, however, and are only meant to make you aware of the dangers of expecting too much too soon. Fortunately, other lines are available that consist of standard or off-the-shelf items. These rarely require as much time to develop as do engineered products and can in fact often be shipped the same day they are ordered. Toys, medical supplies, and many automotive products fall in this category. If you enter a field that deals with these kinds of lines, you can realize commissions in 30 to 60 days after you begin your agency.

Another mistake many prospective representatives make is underestimating the funds needed to support a business. Almost without exception new reps greatly overestimate their first year's sales and underestimate their first year's expenses. The following table,* which shows the yearly cost of running a modest sales agency, is based on an actual case. The sum is formidable, but a beginner can get by on much less. By using an older car and reducing travel and other expenses, he can trim a lot of fat from these figures. But survival is another story. These figures represent only expenses and don't include a penny of income for the representative. Add a modest salary of $10,000 to these costs and you've reached approximately $28,000—the sum needed to meet expenses and keep the wolf from the door for a year.

Advertising and promotion	$ 810
Office expense	780
Phone and Yellow Pages	2,430
Travel, including gas, meals, lodging, and air fares	6,200
Entertainment	800
Postage	500
Dues and subscriptions	275
Professional services	740
Auto lease	2,210
Auto insurance, maintenance, and repairs	1,150
Office rent	1,800
Capital expense	665
	$18,360

Imagine the plight of the newly established representative as he realizes that his nest egg of $25,000 will carry him barely one year into his new profession; and a year is a short time to turn a non-existent entity into a flourishing, or even surviving, business.

The novice in the rep business cannot afford to cut too many cor-

* "A Peek at Your Agent's Finances," *RepLetter,* 1978, p. 1, reprinted with permission.

ners, for without a business that appears to be well financed and successful he will have a difficult time attracting top companies to represent. But there are other reasons why some sales managers, who may personally admire the new enterpreneur in the representative ranks, might hesitate to appoint such a new man. He is, after all, an unknown quantity in a new business. They doubt he has had time to develop a following in that area among purchasing people in companies vital to the sales manager's firm. Moreover, if the rep fails, either by not bringing in new accounts or by going out of business, the failure can be a reflection on the sales manager.

In most cases, then, the top lines are awarded to established sales agencies with visible track records. Sales managers of less successful firms—firms without established business in the representative's territory or with questionable prices, products, and dependability—are more likely to appoint the new man, mainly because they are unable to attract the established professionals.

As the new representative collects these lines and begins to make his rounds, he is confronted by uncertainties he has never faced before. His calls are almost exclusively cold calls made on potential new customers. He's introducing new firms to new buyers, or perhaps old buyers who bought from him when he was a direct-employee salesman. Even in the latter case he finds the going tough. A real roadblock to immediate sales is the buyer's own self-interest. Buyers have to be protective of their positions, regardless of their past relationship with the new representative. They can't afford to go out on a limb simply because an old friend is now representing a new company—a company the buyer has never heard of, or may even have heard bad things about.

These early days can be discouraging. For the new representative there are no more calls on established customers for a cordial lunch and discussion of this year's blanket order, as when he was a direct-employee salesman. Instead, he must conserve his funds and make many calls—many more than he used to—in order to validate the old saying "You've got to make calls if you want to get results." And results often come slowly to the new representative. He has to appear poised and assured, never overeager, at exactly the time when every order is of crucial importance. Self-restraint under these conditions demands extreme self-discipline.

While this is going on, monthly expenses continue; and when many calls are made, expenses rise in relation to activity. More is spent for gas, more for telephone calls following up quotations— funds seem to go out at an alarming rate.

And speaking of travel costs, it is clear that these will escalate rapidly in the future. The rising cost of gas and the sporadic supply problem mean closer attention to trip planning will be required. Of course there is a plus to the fuel crunch. It is one of the main reasons that more firms are turning to reps. When a Los Angeles rep with seven lines travels up the coast to San Francisco he is doing almost the same work as seven direct-employee salesmen, but at one-seventh the cost. Nevertheless, your travel costs will still increase and unfortunately your commissions will probably lag behind.

Life insurance—a common benefit to the direct-employee salesman—may now cost several hundred dollars a year, if not well over a thousand. A company car, previously provided free with maintenance and operating expenses funded by the company, must now be paid for. Perhaps the biggest shock of all comes when the new rep tries to replace his company hospitalization policy by purchasing one with similar benefits. This is when he begins to realize what all those fringe benefits really meant to him. Hospitalization coverage—in any meaningful amount—is prohibitive outside of group plans, and about the only way he can afford it is to work with a high deductible, $750 or more. Even then few companies will cover him for a daily room rate exceeding $30 to $40. In view of present hospital rates, an extended stay could be ruinous.

The new representative will also have to alter his standard of living on the road. As a company salesman or sales manager, he may have been accustomed to staying at first-rate hostelries. In his own business he'll learn to find the smaller, older accommodations that meet his standards of cleanliness and service but can be had for considerably less money. He may have to forgo the conveniences of message services and color TV. Eating habits will undergo some changes, and at the gas station he'll pull into the self-service lane and save several cents a gallon. He may even get used to changing his own oil and oil filter.

In view of all these problems, you may wonder whether any of the novices make it. They certainly do, as we'll find out in succeeding chapters, and most of them do exceptionally well. One friend of mine started with a small base, a very small base. He worked hard—and intelligently—and is now making well over $300,000 a year. Another veteran of my acquaintance makes $100,000 a year. Neither of these is a genius. They are both just good hard workers who took a chance, did the right things, and had some luck.

Others in the field also do well. A survey I recently made of a nationwide group of manufacturers' representatives showed them earning an average of $50,000 per year after expenses. So the rewards are excellent. The money and success are there to be had, but not without some knowledge of how to go about *getting started.*

Unfortunately there are no cut-and-dried formulas, no short cuts or guaranteed procedures to follow to reach success as a professional manufacturers' representative. But there are things that have worked for others, and we'll learn about them from the stories of the men in this book.

My only condition for interviewing these successful representatives was the insistence that actual dollar figures be quoted in outlining their first years in the representative business. I saw no need to identify the firms they represent nor to ask about their present incomes. They are part of the $50,000 average income figure I have already mentioned, and what their individual contribution to this figure amounts to is irrelevant. However, they are all successful representatives and earn an amount sufficient to keep them in business and supplied with the comforts of life.

But the comforts of life can be attained by countless other methods. A man can reach financial comfort within the framework of many organizations—within the ranks of business, industry, or government. So there must be another motivating factor that attracts people to this particular profession. Judging from my interviews with the men whose early experiences are detailed within these pages and my association with numerous other representatives, I'll have to conclude that the independence of the sales rep's lifestyle acts as a magnet to draw men from all types of industries into our profession.

By adhering to the rules and regulations of the corporate game, most of these men could have advanced to relatively comfortable positions in their companies. They could have received the perks and prestige that go with a corporate executive position—a large office with luxurious furnishings, a private secretary, a club membership, and a company car. Then too, the power that goes with an executive position appeals to a large number of corporate workers and sometimes acts as a catalyst for the motivational energies that propel a man who may lack certain executive skills into a top position.

Instead of working toward lofty positions within their companies or industries, however, these men chose the life of the manufacturers' representative, a life where many of the daily working conditions are very different from those in business and industry. A fancy office, for instance, isn't necessary; customers seldom, if ever, visit. Office furnishings should be adequate but not plush. The car used for business purposes must be dependable and economical but need not be a luxury model. Power over associates is nonexistent except in the case where the representative hires an additional salesman; even then the hiring is done for the practical purpose of increasing sales, never for the purpose of practicing power.

The rep's wardrobe must be adequate but not necessarily extensive. He is not forced to purchase a variety of clothing in order to impress his co-workers with his income and status. While making calls he needs to be sensibly dressed, but as an independent salesman, his attire can be more casual than that of a company executive. Nor need he take a two-martini lunch with associates; he can brown-bag it or often he can even go home for the noon break.

It is clear that a manufacturers' representative is really not cut out for a corporate career. All the objects that mark success in the corporation seem to be unimportant to him. Or if they are important, they remain secondary to his extreme drive toward independence.

A background in company affairs, however, will serve him well in his new position, for the rep must deal efficiently and diplomatically with the personnel of his principals. He will recognize the political situations that exist in most companies, and as a result of his previous employment experience, he will practice moderation in working and communicating with the people in the firms he represents.

This awareness of the need for diplomacy in company affairs requires a delicate sensitivity since the independent representative will not be working with only one company but perhaps with as many as ten. Each firm has its own way of doing things. There are situations where management is dictatorial with the sales manager subservient to a capricious owner. Other principals are proponents of the cooperative method of accomplishing sales goals. In still other cases there is little evidence of direction, and the representative virtually has to lead the sales manager in developing sales policies for the representative's area. Since he is not a direct-employee salesman for his principals, he may receive casual treatment from some company personnel when requesting information or urging prompt delivery of a critical component for one of his best customers.

He learns to cooperate with inside personnel who can help him reach his goals of good prices and prompt deliveries. Often a sales correspondent or sales clerk can have more effect on producing results for him than the sales manager himself, who is often out in the field. Even a close liaison with the sales manager's secretary can be helpful. Since the rep is always working from the field, he lacks the day-to-day personal contact that makes communication so much more efficient. Frequently a representative who has become fairly successful, but who has no background in business relations, stumbles in his communication with a principal's personnel. This can cause an underlying animosity within the ranks that could eventually cost him the line.

From the stories in this book—stories of successful men—you'll begin to see that there are common denominators for all potential representatives. You'll discover hints and ideas that could come to you in no other way. Perhaps you have not yet developed the experience factor necessary to begin your own business. In this business, experience comes well after the time it can do you the most good. That is why the methods and techniques followed by our successful examples will be so helpful to you when you are ready to take the big step.

By studying the early careers of these independent commissioned salesmen you'll find that one or two, or possibly several, stories may parallel your own experiences—experiences you had before thinking about entering the independent selling field. Maybe you're an engineer like Paul Rice, motivated to get into sales, but you wonder how to fulfill this desire without prior experience. Perhaps you've been a successful company salesman for many years like Dan Jurgens; now with contacts established and with your wife working, you can finally take those first steps toward starting your own agency.

Sooner or later you'll identify with some of the traits these men possess. Then you may find the will and the way to start out on your own, somewhat secure in the knowledge that someone else has succeeded with similar traits and the will to succeed.

So read on and meet the men who, just as you, have an unquenchable drive for an independent career as a manufacturers' representative.

After you've reviewed one or more techniques that you know will help you get started in the business, I'll take you a little further. You'll also discover modern methods that will produce results when you are trying to line up reputable principals to represent. I'll show you how to identify the companies that will prove to be good principals and how to avoid those that would be a poor risk. I'll also bring you up to date on the latest management procedures practiced by some of the leading sales agencies.

Today's rep is a different breed from his predecessor of a decade or two ago. He's much more professional and entrepreneurial, and often his contacts in the field lead him to new adventures. Several of my rep acquaintances now own manufacturing companies and are appointing reps themselves. Others have done consulting work. Many have seen their agencies grow into large regional sales firms serving some of the top companies in industry. It's not unusual for a division of one of the larger conglomerates to market its products through manufacturers' representatives. When this happens, naturally the services of a large rep firm are required. This is contrary to the popular concept of the manufacturers' representative as a one-man firm operating out of his home.

As you enlarge your business and begin to add personnel, you'll begin to have problems and challenges you couldn't possibly have conceived of when you first opened your agency. Even a one-man firm, however, must face some of these concerns, such as estate problems. In our business it's difficult to build assets because, except for automobiles and office equipment, you have nothing tangible. Goodwill that you've built up over the years is the only thing you have to sell. If you merely leave it to your heirs, it'll be worth nothing. But through careful planning, well ahead of your projected retirement date, you can assure yourself a nice reward when you decide to take it easy or retire.

One of the frustrations I experienced in writing this book came about as a result of my inability to find a woman rep whose story I could tell. At present there are few women in this business; those I've been able to find inherited agencies from their fathers or husbands. In most cases they have increased the fortunes of their business, and this is proof that women can succeed in the rep business. Most women have an even better opportunity than men to begin their own agencies, particularly those whose husbands are employed and can support the family while the wife establishes her agency.

One deterrent pointed out by Georgia Gibson, Operations Director of MANA, is the possibility of the husband being transferred and the agency being dissolved because of the move. However this can be easily overcome if the agency is a successful one and provides a good income. The husband can become more independent and take another local job or join his wife at the agency.

I hope that one of the positive results of this book will be elimination of women's reluctance to enter the rep field. All of the ideas and suggestions presented apply to both sexes, and the field can use the vitality and initiative that today's modern women are capable of contributing.

In the latter chapters of this book, you'll learn all you need to know about running a successful sales agency. Although this book is primarily concerned with getting you off and running as a manufacturers' representative, I don't want to downplay the necessity of good, sound business management. So by the time you reach Chapter 13 you'll feel confident not only of getting a good start in the business but also of being able to run a profitable agency that will mean a happy, satisfying lifestyle and a good income for you.

2
PAUL RICE
From Aeronautical Administration to Manufacturers' Representative

RELAXING IN HIS comfortable office in Dallas, Paul Rice seems the typical well-paid, secure corporate executive. His office building, just off North Central Expressway, is in an area boasting numerous high-rise office complexes housing insurance companies, banks, and even a Playboy Club.

The afternoon I visited Paul he was a picture of prosperity, wearing a handsome vested suit, sporting a well-trimmed mustache, and completely at ease in his office surroundings. Later when we lunched at a nearby restaurant, Paul passed the time of day with several business acquaintances while we waited for a table. All in all, he represented what I considered the image of a successful corporate man who had arrived and was enjoying his position and the benefits that accompanied it.

But Paul is not a corporate executive. He's a manufacturers' representative—and a good one.

[14]

Despite appearances, Paul is a hard worker and is seldom in his office between 9:00 A.M. and 4:30 P.M. He's usually out of town for one or two weeks during the average month. While he is not a *corporate* executive, Paul is nevertheless an executive. His firm is Paul Rice & Associates, a common device used in our business to allow for expansion of the firm and to indicate more than a one-man agency. Paul, however, is still a one-man agency. As president, sales manager, controller, and advertising manager of his company, he is more versatile and effective than the average corporate executive who usually concentrates on one specialty.

But it was not always so. Paul is just now reaping the benefits of years of hard work in the rep business, and the road was strenuous and rocky. His entrepreneurial instinct—a common trait among successful reps—eventually paid off. Today he is well on the way toward an attractive income, self-sufficiency, and a smoothly operating rep sales agency.

Paul was born in Chicago, but a short time later his family moved to Shelbyville, Tennessee, where he was raised. His father was a career military man who, although he moved from base to base during his time in the service, insisted that his children be reared in one location. So Paul and his two sisters remained in Shelbyville until they finished high school. Paul had always been mechanically minded and fascinated with the aviation industry, and so he decided to major in aeronautical engineering. Being outgoing and gregarious, he gradually came to realize that, as an engineer in the aviation industry, his opportunities to meet other people would be somewhat limited. He foresaw his working environment as a room with four walls and a drawing board. Early in his college studies, after recognizing the probability of an unhappy vocational future, Paul changed his major to aeronautical administration. His new curriculum included some engineering studies but focused on managerial techniques. Although he chose the administration wing of the aviation industry, he sensed that his real desire was to have a sales position in that industry.

As company recruiters visited his campus, Paul made plain his desire to join one of the major companies in a sales position. In 1962 the aviation-industry recruiters were eager to hire engineers and administrators straight out of school. Almost to a man, however, they had nothing to offer in the way of entry-level sales positions. Had Paul had some previous sales experience, there would have been opportunities at several companies. Without such experience, his talents were not in demand.

Discouraged but unwilling to give up, Paul accepted a position in engineering administration with the Vought Corporation, which is now part of the LTV empire. He started working at Vought's Grand Prairie, Texas, plant promptly after graduation. He liked the work—it was a fine vehicle for his technical background—but he didn't care for the environment. Although he had been hired for the administrative segment of the engineering department, he still had to put in apprentice time on the drawing board. The unappealing prospect of continuing on this basis for several years filled him with frustration. But it was a good job, and it paid for the groceries.

Somewhere along the line of every successful rep's career, fate seems to step in and provide an opportunity for diversion into the rep field. In Paul's case it wasn't exactly a welcome event. The fortunes of most aerospace companies are tied directly to government contracts; and in 1964 LTV's share of the government pie was sliced rather thin, with predictable results—layoffs in most departments. Paul's tenure with the firm was brief, and so he was one of the first to receive the unpleasant news. He found himself, two years out of school, out of a job.

Still determined to get into sales work, he started interviewing for positions that would enable him to enter this field and also utilize his mechanical skills and knowledge. In response to a newspaper ad, he made an appointment with a manufacturers' representative in the mechanical-component field who needed a salesman to handle part of his growing business. At that point Paul didn't even know what a manufacturers' representative was, but an opportunity was an opportunity, so he kept his appointment.

As he trudged up to the second floor of an older building on a side street in north Dallas, he became apprehensive. But when he entered the dingy office, he became downright discouraged. Having been used to the plush surroundings at Vought, he couldn't understand how someone with such a small and ill-equipped office could even think of putting on an extra man. From appearances the rep was having a hard time supporting himself, let alone another employee. What Paul didn't know was that he was visiting one of the most successful reps in the Dallas area.

The interview went well and the rep, obviously impressed with Paul's technical background, offered him a position at a starting salary of $650 per month plus expenses and a car. In 1964 this was a reasonable income for a beginner. In addition, the job would provide Paul an opportunity to learn the rep business—a real advantage but one he didn't fully appreciate or understand at the time. Still unimpressed, Paul asked for a day to think over the job offer, although he had his mind pretty well made up against joining a firm that apparently was in a strange business and that, on appearance, didn't have much to recommend it.

That evening he had dinner with a friend, a salesman to whom he related the incident. His friend patiently explained what a manufacturers' representative does for a living and how he makes his money. He told Paul stories of several successful reps he knew, pointing out that reps never have customers visit their offices and so worry little about appearance. Because of this, the friend explained, over half of all reps work from their homes. He concluded by saying that if Paul didn't accept the job, he would go after it himself.

Heartened by his friend's appraisal, which he knew was sincere, Paul arrived bright and early the next morning at the rep's office and accepted the job. Even then he didn't realize the attractive opportunity that lay ahead of him. ·

That he had made a good impression on the rep was evident when Paul accepted the job, because the rep turned to his secretary and said, "Call the young man who's due at 11:00 A.M. and tell him the job's been filled." On the surface, the hiring of Paul by the rep didn't make much sense. Although he had always been interested in sales, Paul didn't have one hour of sales experience—a shortcoming that would have made an average employer think twice about putting him on the payroll. Sales experience is even more essential in the rep business where the whole purpose of hiring a new man is to have him start selling from day one. Reps seldom can afford the luxury of training a man to sell in addition to teaching him the product line.

But Paul's employer was no novice. He had been in the selling business for a long time. He recognized that enthusiasm makes up for a lot of experience, and he saw that Paul naturally exuded enthusiasm. The employer also realized that a man with an engineering background had a lot going for him. He knew that technical training could be an invaluable asset to a salesman who would be trying to convince engineers and buyers in prospective customers' plants of the technical superiority of his companies' products. And he reasoned that Paul's enthusiasm would gradually be converted to a professional approach.

Paul admits that for the first few months he was filled with apprehension whenever he drove into the parking lot of a prospective customer's plant, not an unusual feeling for a raw trainee. But after eight or ten months on the job this feeling was replaced by a new sense of confidence based on a knowledge of his principals' products and his ability to present those products to potential buyers in a manner guaranteed to spark their interest. And he had begun to establish new business for his boss, business from companies that hadn't bought from the agency before.

Paul continued to improve his skills and four years later was making $750 a month. He was happy in his job and with his lifestyle until, as he put it, "The boss's daughter got married." I asked him what bearing such a happy event could possibly have had on his employment status. He replied, "I was promptly replaced by the new son-in-law." He added, with a chuckle, "Now when I look back I realize how stupid I was. She was a beautiful girl, but the thought of courting her didn't occur to me. I guess I put business before pleasure . . . and common sense."

Paul was back on the street, but not for long. With four years of good, solid sales experience behind him, he quickly found a job with another rep. This was a larger operation employing four salesmen to cover the Southwest and stocking many of its companies' products in its Dallas warehouse. The agency owner, a self-made man who had started his business from scratch, was a good salesman and manager but not a particularly pleasant person to work for, which is often the case in smaller agencies and companies. But Paul persevered and traveled the Dallas–Ft. Worth–East Texas area for his new employer.

For the first time since his entry into the field, Paul started to pay serious attention to sales records. Because he had always worked on a straight-salary basis—he was under this arrangement with his new employer—he had been only casually interested in the overall sales figures of the agency. No bonus or commissions accrued from his sales efforts. But now he became curious and since the records were available to him, he examined them closely. He promptly noticed that his assigned territory had provided excellent sales volume by the end of the first year, particularly when compared with the previous year's meager results. He could see that he was contributing substantially to the agency's income.

Five years after his first sales call the light finally went on. "Why," he asked himself, "am I doing all this work and helping make someone else wealthy while I go along with a modest income? I could be working just as hard in my own business and keeping the lion's share for myself." Adding fuel to the fire was, no doubt, his unhappiness with his employer, which he attributes to a personality conflict.

From these humble beginnings, as they say, rose a new rep firm, Paul Rice & Associates.

At that point the only positive assets that the new firm possessed were Paul Rice himself and a firm name, Paul Rice & Associates—not a tremendous foundation from which to launch a new business. Paul, like most of us, lived up to his income. He had little savings, no home to mortgage, and owed money on his car. Fortunately, however, he had no large debts and was single, with no responsibility for supporting anyone but himself. Being unmarried was a somewhat unusual advantage. Most fledgling reps have families to support and worry about when they need to be able to concentrate all their energies on establishing their sales agencies.

Still, with no obvious assets, Paul wasn't in an enviable position. There was simply no way he could begin on his own without a backer or without going substantially into debt. He found few lending institutions interested in backing a new entrepreneur, especially one with no previous experience in running his own business.

It finally dawned on Paul that if he was really serious about his own agency he would have to make a greater-than-normal sacrifice, and he began to plan for his entrance into the rep ranks.

His first move after saying good-bye to his employer was to obtain an ordinary laborer's job on a short evening shift, weekdays, at a local factory. This was dirty and tiring work, but it fitted his plan. His hours were from 6:00 P.M. to 10:00 P.M. The 6:00 P.M. starting time was conveniently after conventional working hours, and by quitting at 10:00 P.M. he could still get a good night's sleep.

Income from this job was only a partial contribution to the total amount he needed; so his next step was to find a weekend job. After considerable thought and searching, Paul came upon the ideal opportunity—a weekend job at a car-rental agency.

Several advantages to this job, which were not apparent at first glance, fitted in perfectly with his needs. For one thing the job was for weekends only, which meant it wouldn't encroach on his selling time; nor would it interfere with his nightly chores at the factory. Another real plus lay in the fact that car-rental agencies are notoriously inactive on the weekend since their major customer, the traveling businessman, seldom needs a car during that period. Thus the job was practically a caretaker operation, and Paul had little to do except show up and make sure the phone was answered and the occasional customer serviced. This gave him the entire weekend to concentrate on starting and maintaining his new agency, at least as far as his paperwork obligations were concerned. He could also use the rental agency's auto-maintenance facilities to keep his car in shape at little personal cost—a major plus.

Paul's total income from both jobs was $450 per month—not a magnificent sum, but sufficient for him to live on and maintain his agency on a modest basis. But even with this continuing income

Paul didn't have an active agency since he had no lines—no companies to represent—and without these he had nothing to sell.

He promptly set about remedying this situation. His business philosophy prevented him from soliciting the lines represented by his former employers, and so he made use of business directories and trade journals to find prospective principals to work for. He tried to be selective and chose only those companies whose products were compatible with the products he had formerly sold. This was a judicious move. By lining up with a company that made products similar to those he had previously sold and was familiar with, he could go back to customers he had developed over the preceding five years with confidence and effectiveness.

Paul wrote approximately 30 letters a month. Most of the companies that replied indicated they already had representation or that they weren't interested in his market. But about two months after he began writing to these firms he received his first appointment; gradually, over the ensuing months, he picked up several more. These early companies were not exactly the cream of the crop. By and large they were smaller firms that figured it wouldn't hurt to have someone making calls for them in Texas. It didn't cost them anything until a sale was made—an attitude that was reflected in their servicing of Paul's area. There were, however, one or two diamonds in the rough, and Paul was able to begin building his business on the basis of these few capable companies.

With his days free, Paul could make calls at regular hours on his former customers in the Dallas–Ft. Worth area, and little by little orders started to trickle in. Eight months after his entry into the rep business, he received his first commission check—for $38. It wasn't a large amount, but it was solid evidence to Paul that he was in business.

During these early stages, and to this day, Paul used the services of a local mailing and answering firm. This gave him a business address and phone even though at first he wasn't physically located there. Working from his home, he held expenses to a minimum. Later he rented offices adjacent to the answering service, making communication with customers and principals more convenient and effective.

At the end of 1970, his first year in business, Paul added up his commission receipts and found he had earned the grand total of $504. This worked out to be a little more than $40 per month for each month he had been in business. By then, however, he had received larger additional orders that would be shipped in 1971, and he knew that he would be receiving larger checks in a few months. Banking on these commissions, Paul felt he could now afford to leave his weekly night shift at the factory. It was beginning to wear on him since he was becoming much more active in the daytime. So he resigned the factory job but still kept his weekend job at the car-rental agency.

By no longer working at night, Paul was able to take short overnight trips into parts of his territory he hadn't previously visited as Paul Rice & Associates. These were areas where he had contacts developed while working for his previous employers. This increased his potential marketplace considerably, and he quickly overcame the loss of income he had experienced by leaving the factory job.

At the end of 1971, his second full year in business, Paul again added up his commissions. This time the total came to over $5,000. He was firmly established in his own business and on his way to a successful career as a manufacturers' representative.

In his third year in the rep business, Paul was progressing at a very happy pace. He was opening more accounts for his better principals and was also upgrading his list of lines. Early in any rep's career he takes on lines out of necessity, or even desperation, and values quantity over quality. But as he becomes more established and attempts to become more selective, he improves the overall quality of the companies he represents. This may sound like an irresponsible attitude, but you must remember that most lines a rep begins with appoint him because they have no existing business in the area and are unable to sign up the successful veteran reps. As the new rep becomes more professional in his operation, he will attract more of the reputable and established lines. This is not to say that reps abandon all their early lines. In many instances, where they have succeeded with these lines, they are only too happy to continue their association with companies that have proved responsive to them and their customer's needs.

At this point it might have been reasonable to assume that Paul would also relinquish his weekend job with the car-rental agency. But having no marital obligations, he found the advantages of the job outweighed the free time he would have gained if he had left the agency. So he stayed on, using the time on the job to continue servicing his car and to complete paperwork chores for his sales agency. The car-rental firm didn't object to these activities as long as they didn't infringe on his sporadic duties—and they didn't.

At the end of the third year in his own rep business, Paul again added up his total commissions and found that 1972 had produced over $10,000. Added to this amount was the income from his weekend job—not bad for a single man in his own growing business. At this time Paul got married. His overall situation was improved with the $850 per month that his bride contributed to the household coffers.

It was time at last to say good-bye to the car-rental agency, which he did. He was now a full-time, self-supporting, honest-to-goodness manufacturers' representative. It appeared Paul had gone through the obligatory trial period and had succeeded. But there was a detour down the road.

During one of his sales trips into Arkansas, he was dismayed to learn that a large potential customer for one of his products had been buying from another Dallas rep for years and had little intention of changing. As an afterthought, the buyer mentioned that the Dallas rep was getting toward retirement age and was actively looking for a younger partner to take over his agency. Perhaps a little too aggressively, Paul pursued the comment. He thought that, by seeking out this apparent opportunity, he might be able to accelerate his rise in the rep profession. So immediately upon his return to Dallas he phoned the other rep, told him what he had heard, and asked if he was interested in talking about a merger or buy-out. The older rep was most certainly interested, and they arranged for a meeting. This initial contact turned into a six months' negotiation.

The older rep's assets were larger and consisted of more established lines. Paul's contribution would be youthful enthusiasm backed by eight years of solid experience in the rep business, both as an employed salesman and as the owner of a rep agency with a substantial following in compatible products.

In the following six months they met often to work out a fair and understandable arrangement for a merger of the two agencies. The agreement they signed had the following terms: Paul would give up all his competitive lines, which meant he would bring only one line into the new company and resign the rest. In return, all expenses would be paid out of gross commissions of the agency. What was left would be split 80–20 percent at the end of the first year with the older rep receiving the larger percentage. The same practice would be followed in each ensuing year except that the percentage would change each year. The second-year split would be 70–30, the third year 60–40, and so on until Paul became the sole owner and beneficiary of the profits.

It turned out that after the first year's split, Paul's 20 percent would be almost double his income at that time. Consequently, he was extremely happy with this arrangement and entered the merger adventure with unbounded enthusiasm. The older rep was also happy with his new partner and the chance to share the responsibility of running a busy rep agency. At least he was happy for the first year.

However, at the end of the second year with a 70–30 split of the proceeds, the threat of his share of the agency's income continuing to diminish alarmed the older rep to a greater degree than he wished. Paul conjectures that this fear was so overwhelming (although the older man was financially well-off) that he couldn't bear to continue their arrangement. So after two and a half years he abruptly informed Paul he wished to dissolve their partnership and return to his former status of a one-man agency.

Paul was stunned. Since he had given up all but one of his lines as a condition of the merger, he was practically back where he had started five years earlier, a rep with only one line. His associate softened the blow by promising Paul a second line that, together with the line he would retain, would allow him sufficient income to survive until he was able to rebuild his business. But even that hope was dashed on moving day when the older rep told Paul he had decided to retain the line.

Ironically, because the older man had such a fine business when the merger was made, Paul had had every intention of never letting the split fall below 50–50. He had neglected to tell the rep of his intentions because he had planned it as a pleasant surprise at the proper moment. Now it was too late. To mention the matter would have been interpreted as an insincere attempt to continue the association. Though Paul accepted the break with equanimity, it was not without some bitterness at his being denied the promised line that would have made life easier.

During his partnership with the older rep, Paul and his wife had come to a parting of the ways. While he again had no family obligations, he also had very little income since he was completely dependent upon his one remaining line. His good reputation and rapport with his customers were exceptionally helpful in this down time of his career. Within months he found another good line, and with it he was able to recoup some of his income.

The new company fortuitously scheduled a sales meeting shortly after he signed up with it, and Paul took off for Chicago to attend. During coffee breaks and in the evening, he had the opportunity to meet and visit with some of the other reps with the company. He told several of them about his situation, and one or two were able to refer him to their principals who were looking for good representation in the Texas market.

Within a year Paul was back in business in a real sense. He had recovered and was again making a good income. His ace in the hole was his relationships with a host of customers he had sold and serviced over a ten-year period as an employee, a rep, a partner in a rep firm, and again as an independent rep.

These ups and downs have helped Paul mature considerably, and his future outlook is good. Many a man without the tenacity of Paul Rice would have given up long ago. Instead Paul has clung to his fierce desire to succeed in the rep business. He has six strong lines that he enthusiastically represents and is looking toward the day he can expand his agency.

In thinking about the growth of his agency, Paul realizes that problems similar to those he has already experienced may again confront him. There is just so much one man can do, just so many calls he can make. In a particularly good marketing area, by himself he will not be able to take advantage of all the potential that exists.

Paul has already been turned down by three companies he wanted badly to represent, because those firms insisted upon an agency with more than one salesman. This is frustrating to him but he's aware of the problems that can arise when he seeks to add sales personnel and is probably subconsciously putting off that day. He does admit, however, that if he obtains a line that has, or promises, a potential beyond his capabilities, he will definitely add one or more salesmen to his agency. But the implementation of this plan is still vague in his mind and will probably remain so until the actual need confronts him.

In the meantime Paul is truly happy in his work, has married again, and is convinced that his work and lifestyle will continue to prove extremely satisfying.

ANALYSIS

To the aspiring representative, Paul Rice's technique for establishing his own rep agency may be unappetizing. The long hours of part-time work hardly fit the image of success, and the apprenticeship he served working for other reps may appear to have been a waste of time.

But Paul's method had two very important advantages. First, by working in a realistic rep environment without putting up his own money, he was able to learn all facets of the business. He discovered how to impress principals and customers, found how to obtain lines, and became knowledgeable about the characteristics necessary to be his own man. The second and more important advantage was that when he struck out on his own he never had to face the urgent need to reach breakeven day—the day when expenses would finally be equaled by commission income. His part-time jobs provided a sufficient, though not substantial, living. He could have continued for years, had it been necessary, on this basis because he had theoretically reached breakeven day when he started his agency.

To one entering the rep business with a capital investment derived from the sale of assets (such as a home) but without a continuing income from another source, breakeven day is a very important factor. The money can well run out before that day arrives, and all the effort and sacrifice can count for nothing.

Paul's determination to succeed quickly perhaps led to a delay in reaching his present status. Sensing a real opportunity to get ahead faster, he joined forces with the older rep. That their association didn't work out was not Paul's fault, and even today he feels it was worth it. But it did slow him down. Seasoned reps caution against such a move. Partnerships are often tenuous, and the differing goals of partners can lead to the destruction of a partnership. Surely this happened in Paul's case, but he learned a valuable lesson.

This doesn't mean that he won't again enter into a partnership arrangement to expand his agency or to provide more security for himself in the event of a disability. But the next time he decides to look into such an association, he will be better equipped to insist on much more attractive terms, just as the older rep did with him.

Without the experience of his partnership problem, Paul might have entered into a future agreement without sufficient guarantee of solvency for himself. That won't happen now.

The story of Paul Rice amply demonstrates one excellent method for entering the manufacturers' representative business. It is not without sacrifice, but Paul has no feelings of regret and would willingly do it all over again to gain the success and self-satisfaction he enjoys today.

3
DICK COLE
Opportunity in the Valley of the Sun

MANY OF US work hard all year so we can take a few weeks' vacation to relax and enjoy the luxuries of a resort area. Those whose incomes are higher than average may even spend these few weeks at a popular winter resort such as Phoenix, Arizona. After that, however, it's back to the colder climes of Chicago, Cleveland, or Philadelphia.

A fortunate few are able to live in these winter resorts, not on pensions or Social Security, but in pursuit of an active career with a handsome income. One of these lucky people is Dick Cole, a 48-year-old manufacturers' representative who lives in Phoenix.

There is, of course, no free lunch, and Dick Cole works hard, often leaving his home Sunday morning in order to arrive at his destination in time to begin selling early on Monday. However, after only three years as a rep his energetic schedule is beginning to pay off. Soon his working life will return to a more normal schedule, and eventually Dick expects to become more of an administrator than a salesman.

As a young man in Cleveland, Ohio, Dick Cole had no plans to become a manufacturers' representative; he didn't even know what the term meant. When he was in high school, his father entered the construction and land-development business. The venture was successful, and it was natural for Dick's father to assume Dick would later join him in the business.

Realizing that a degree in architecture would be an asset in the construction business, Dick—when he was ready to enter college—investigated the prerequisites for a career as an architect. He found, somewhat tardily, that he should have taken more courses in geometry and algebra in high school. Instead he had concentrated on subjects that catered to his artistic bent, watercolors and oil painting.

Dick's lack of concentration on math practically ruled out further plans for an architectural degree; so he majored in fine arts with a minor in political science at Miami University in Miami, Ohio. His fine arts studies didn't interfere with his intentions to go into business with his father after graduation from college. As a matter of fact, it turned out that his artistic ability later played a major role in his taking a job that ultimately led to his career as a rep.

Dick started helping his father in the construction business during summer vacations. While at school he would trot back to Cleveland on weekends to assist in the sale of homes at his father's model-home display.

The Korean War erupted when Dick was in college, and immediately upon graduation he was drafted into the army. His major and minor studies served him well during his tour of duty. On the basis of his knowledge of political science, he obtained an assignment as a test instructor and performed duties in troop education and information. In this function training aids were an important adjunct, and Dick, with his artistic capabilities, was able to design and construct the required aids.

Upon leaving the service in 1958, Dick found his father disenchanted with life and work in Cleveland and looking toward warmer climates. He owned some property in the Phoenix area and suggested that Dick move there, manage the property, and prepare the groundwork for starting a construction business in Phoenix. Unattached and eager to begin his career, Dick packed up and moved west. He settled down in Phoenix and went to work as a real estate broker to learn the market in anticipation of his father's arrival and the start-up of their construction business.

While winding down his affairs in the Cleveland area, Dick's father began to have second thoughts about committing his hard-earned savings to a new business in an unfamiliar market. By the time he arrived in Phoenix, his doubts had solidified into real opposition to the idea. He stayed for about a year and then moved on to California. There he purchased a small gift shop, which required a lot less investment than the $100,000 it would have taken to get into the Phoenix construction market.

Dick, in the meantime, wasn't exactly setting the world on fire in the real estate business. He feels he could have prospered had he been willing to engage in some of the doubtful practices that were rampant in the Arizona real estate market in the fifties, but he had no stomach for such shenanigans. He stayed honest—and poor.

While wondering what to do to improve his standard of living, Dick met Sharon Marcus. He also met her father who, it turned out, was indirectly responsible for Dick's ultimate career as a rep. When Dick and Sharon decided to get married in 1960, Mr. Marcus gently informed Dick that he wasn't too keen on his daughter's marrying a real estate broker. As a matter of fact, he was downright against it and strongly suggested that if parental approval was to be forthcoming, Dick should get a respectable job.

Dick studied the newspaper's want-ad sections the day after Mr. Marcus's ultimatum and saw an advertisement for a salesman placed by one of the country's major game manufacturers. When he applied for the job, he learned the company needed someone to sell games to commercial accounts and also to handle another line—art supplies—that would be sold to schools.

Again Dick's artistic talents came into play. He readily obtained the job, since selling art supplies was a natural for him, and he could easily learn the game business. In other parts of the country his company had a man for each product line, but the mountain states were so sparsely populated at that time that Dick's new employer counted on him to do double duty and hired him on that basis—another lucky break for Dick on his journey toward his rep career. Had he sold only art supplies, he probably wouldn't have become involved in the game end of his company's business, which now makes up a major portion of his income.

Dick married Sharon in 1960 and began selling for his new employer in Arizona. As the years went by his successes mounted and his territory was enlarged. First it was El Paso, Texas, and New Mexico, then Colorado, Utah, Nevada, Wyoming, and Montana. Later he also sold to a couple of national retailers in his area.

Naturally Dick's traveling became more and more extensive as the years went by and his territory grew. In his business it was imperative that samples of the company's games be shown to prospective buyers. Since that ruled out air travel, he would load up his Chevy sedan with samples and set out for the far reaches of his territory. In the last few years with the game manufacturer, he averaged 40,000 miles of driving yearly.

After 15 years of hard work Dick knew buyers, in large and small businesses alike, all over his territory and had made many good friends. Back in 1960 when he started with the company, sales in the mountain states had been running about $50,000 a year. By 1975 Dick had brought this to $1.5 million, an attractive volume for one man who was costing his company only $28,000 a year in salary plus expenses.

Evidently, as Dick discovered later, a younger, less experienced man at $10,000 or $12,000 a year would make the territory even more profitable to the company, and he attributes his abrupt dismissal in May 1975 to this philosophy. No particular justification was given, just a good-bye notice from his sales manager. When Dick was applying for another job shortly thereafter, an employment-agency counselor received an excellent recommendation for him from his company. When the counselor asked why Dick had been let go, he was informed that the company was able to hire a younger man at a cost considerably less than Dick's $28,000.

Part of his settlement with his employer was the company's agreement to provide truthful references to future potential employers or, as it turned out in Dick's case, prospective principals.

A few years prior to leaving this company, Dick had felt the need to make more income. The cost of living in Phoenix is among the highest in the United States, and although Dick was making $25,000 to $28,000 a year, it was hard to live comfortably on that income in an area where millionaires go to play.

As a result he purchased, with a partner investor, a small toy store that netted approximately $10,000 a year. The partners later purchased a second store and, in both cases, appointed managers to run the stores.

The combination of absentee management and the booming popularity of the *major mall* concept (Dick's stores were in *minor* centers in the Phoenix area) soon had an effect on the stores' profits, and they began to lose money. When Dick lost his job, he realized he couldn't go on suffering these setbacks, so he sold out, at a loss, to his partner. This brought in a small amount of immediate cash.

Before his dismissal, Dick had sensed that his status with his company was changing but hadn't been exactly sure what was happening. Because of this uneasiness he had refinanced his house. As it happened, this was a timely decision, because he was released just a few months later. As a result of the sale of the toy stores and the refinancing of his home, along with some small savings, Dick found himself with about $18,000 in cash at the time of his dismissal.

His first reaction was to seek employment with another company. He watched the newspapers for job ads and visited employment agencies. Although he received job offers from other game manufacturers, he knew that he didn't want to go through that experience again.

Dick had known a few reps in the toy business but had never seriously thought about getting into it himself. Now with job pickings not entirely satisfactory and with the prospect of his nest egg diminishing at a rapid rate, he decided to become a manufacturers' representative. On January 1, 1976, Dick Cole established his business—Richard H. Cole—with lots of potential customers and one principal.

How did he get that one principal? Through a tough three-day session with the company's owner.

When he decided to open his own agency, Dick contacted a West Coast game manufacturer with an excellent reputation but with poor sales—only $10,000 a year—in the mountain states. Dick sought out this particular man because of his fine reputation, both as an individual and as the president of a potentially good-volume principal.

The two men spent three days together going over Dick's qualifications. Dick faced the same problem that most new reps face. Good principals are reluctant to award their lines to a man just starting out because he may fail, and all the groundwork the company has provided will then go to waste. The game company president was concerned that Dick might become discouraged and accept one of the offers he had received from other game manufacturers.

Dick, on the other hand, wanted the line desperately since he knew he could quickly parlay the $10,000—at 10 percent commission—into a major line.

After those three days of discussion and soul-searching, the president awarded Dick the line. It turned out to be a mutually beneficial arrangement: In the first year, as he predicted, Dick sold $50,000 worth of the company's games; in the second year this almost doubled, reaching a volume of $90,000.

Dick felt that one of the reasons he had such a difficult time convincing the president to award him the line was because he didn't have the look of a professional—no calling cards, stationery, or office. He feels strongly that if he were to begin all over again he would be professionally prepared before even thinking about soliciting his first line. However, he promptly remedied this lack of professionalism by obtaining the necessary business supplies, although he continued working from his home and still does so today.

With only one line, Dick realized that his position was far from secure and that it would be necessary to quickly solicit and sign up additional principals. His initial line would bring him only a portion of his business expenses and none of his living expenses. So Dick put Sharon to work.

She hauled out their typewriter, and over a period of two months she wrote over 1,000 letters to game and toy manufacturers. Dick had composed a standard letter telling of his background with his former employer, but he individualized it somewhat, depending on what he knew about the company he was writing to. If the company sold to volume discount chains, he would emphasize his experience in that field. If the company wanted to sell to exclusive toy stores, he would point out his background in that segment of the market.

He also used a unique approach to references. He told his prospective principals to call *any* toy store in the mountain states and ask about him. These principals were astounded at this blanket approach to references, but Dick was willing to take his chances on that basis. Because he had been so thorough in covering his territory, it wasn't often that a principal found a buyer who didn't know Dick Cole.

In each case Dick directed his letter to the president of the company, not the sales manager. While I wouldn't ordinarily suggest this approach in other industries, it worked exceptionally well for Dick. He received responses from almost all the companies he wrote to, some indicating interest and some not. Others asked him to get in touch with them in a year or so. By the time the annual toy convention—Toy Fair—rolled around in February, Dick had signed up four additional principals. He also replied to those who had given a positive response to his original letter, and he arranged for appointments during Toy Fair, which is held each year in New York City.

He dug deep into his reserves to afford the trip to New York, but the expense was well worth the effort. He picked up several more lines during his two-week stay. The trip also gave him a chance to visit with many of the buyers from the mountain states who were

attending the convention and to tell them he would soon be calling
on them as a manufacturers' representative.

Some of these buyers and owners, old friends of Dick's from his
previous 15 years of selling, even recommended him to certain other
manufacturers, unsolicited. Several went so far as to advise certain
manufacturers with no reps in the mountain states that they would
prefer to make their purchases through Dick Cole. It naturally followed that Dick was appointed on the spot by several companies
who were later delighted with a relationship that had initially appeared somewhat forced. Naturally, in shotgun marriages such as
these, some work out and some don't, but a number of good ones
stuck.

While still with his old employer, Dick had helped a small toy
chain receive a national line of credit with his company, a great
help to the president of the firm. When Dick phoned the toy-chain
president to say he was going into his own business, the man immediately sent a memo to all his stores. These stores had dramatically
increased in number since the early days, and the president told his
buyers to extend extra courtesies to Dick and, whenever possible, to
give him an order.

One big advantage for Dick in his early days of obtaining lines
was the amazing lack of knowledge among prospective principals of
the potential market in the mountain states. Many of them sold as
far west as Chicago or maybe even Kansas City. Then they skipped
from these midwestern states to California, completely ignoring the
Denver area with a population of almost a million and a half and
the Phoenix area with well over a million. Further, several chains
with over a hundred stores each are *based* in these two cities. Since
most companies did not have reps in the mountain states, they had
nothing to lose by appointing Dick.

Through his acquaintances in the business, Dick knew which
lines good reps around the country were carrying, and he made a
special point to contact the companies these reps worked for. If a
line was being carried by a mountain states rep, Dick adopted a
hands-off policy. But in some cases reps based in California didn't

bother to visit his area more than once or twice a year. They carried certain lines simply because no one in the mountain states bothered to. When the line was a good one Dick took it on, if asked, simply because he knew he could move the goods better than someone who seldom entered the territory.

Through these early stages, Sharon played an important part in building the business. She decided that Dick should carry a line of children's records and told him so. He tactfully informed her there was one company that dominated the field and that it would be the only one he would consider handling. He also predicted that because this firm was so large, it would have its own direct-employee salesman covering the area.

Sharon agreed that he was probably right, but a few weeks later Dick received a letter from that large record firm offering him its line. Sharon's intuition and initiative had won over Dick's professional knowledge. She had written a letter, on her own, to the company, and it *didn't* have anyone in the area and therefore offered Dick the opportunity to be its representative.

The rest of this story is indicative of the professionalism of Dick Cole. As he does with all prospective lines, he went out and attempted to sell the company's recordings. Eight stores ordered their original assortment of records from him, which amounted to about $700 per store. With his letter of acceptance to the record company, he included orders for over $5,000 worth of business. He was promptly phoned by the astonished sales manager, who said he'd never had this happen before and was extremely pleased with the new association.

Dick's policy of sending orders along with his letter of acceptance has a more tangible aim than simply impressing the sales manager. In the game and toy business, it's possible to receive a very quick reaction from buyers about the salability of a particular item. If Dick can't obtain a few orders as a result of his first rounds, he may want to decline the line. This is a luxury that those of us in engineered products don't have. When pioneering a new line, months usually pass before we know whether a given line will sell.

Dick has a large customer in Phoenix he calls on whenever he receives the offer of a new line. If that firm expresses doubts about purchasing the toys or games of the new company, he is then very hesitant about spending time on it. He has found through experience that if his large Phoenix customer won't buy a line, he'll have even more trouble with smaller stores.

Although Dick is fortunate in being somewhat able to forecast the success of a line in advance, his business has a disadvantage that perhaps reps in most other industries do not experience. Aside from a few solid, growing principals, Dick's companies are mostly small firms; in such a competitive field many go out of business, some overnight. Therefore Dick's lines change more often than those of most reps.

Dick must constantly be on the lookout for new firms to represent. If he isn't, attrition will soon set in leaving him with only a few lines. By attending Toy Fair every year, he is able to keep tabs on what's happening in the toy and game industry. And, of course, it gives him an opportunity to carefully watch the financial health of his current firms. Toy Fair is also the ideal place to become aware of any new entries into the field that would make logical principals for him.

During the first six months Dick Cole was in business, he spent $10,000 in expenses and took in $2,000. This loss was not unusual for a beginning rep, since a large portion of the early months is normally spent finding good principals. Dick had good principals after just a few months, but he made one error. He thought the best way to introduce his sales agency to old friends would be to set up a temporary showroom in each major town he visited. He would then invite the buyers to come in and view his complete line of toys and games. This didn't work. Buyers apparently were too busy to leave their stores, and Dick found that sales weren't going well.

He quickly abandoned this approach and thereafter visited the stores in person to sell his goods. His orders began to pick up, but his nest egg began to disappear. By September 1976 Dick's $18,000 had dwindled to a mere $500, hardly enough to run a business—let alone feed his family of five.

Fortunately Dick had excellent relations with his banker because he had promptly paid off the loans he negotiated for the purchase of the two toy stores. He took his order book to the bank to show how the orders were coming in and to indicate that a fair amount of goods on which commissions were due had already been shipped.

The bank offered him a substantial loan, but Dick borrowed only $4,000, which he felt would get him through his temporary cash-flow problem. He was right. By the end of the year he had received approximately $25,000 in commissions, an excellent start.

Dick also learned that he could negotiate commissions with some of his companies. He averages 10 percent, which is higher than normal in his industry. This is because of the unusually high expense involved in covering the mountain states. When I visited him, he had put 18,000 miles on his car in the previous three months. He does an excellent and thorough job for all of his lines; he also entertains a lot and sends out a considerable number of mailings. Under these circumstances, he feels he needs a higher commission rate than reps in more concentrated areas of the country. His principals agree.

In 1977 Dick's hard work began to pay off. More companies called him asking if he would like to represent them, and by the end of that year he had grossed approximately $55,000.

Also, unbeknown to him he was selling some of his lines in larger volumes than they were being sold on the West Coast. Several of these companies approached him, wanting him to cover California for them if he would open an office there. Dick had no desire to enlarge his operation to include the West Coast, but Sharon's brother was interested in leaving his employer for greener fields. When Dick asked his brother-in-law if he wanted to get into the toy business, he readily agreed, and within ten days had set up shop in California with six good lines.

Dick made no attempt to form a partnership or to have a financial stake in the business, because he felt this might cause problems. However, each agency works as an extension of the other. When one obtains a good line to represent, he refers it to the other, thereby strengthening both agencies. They exhibit together at the California toy show, and this loose association works out well for both Dick and his brother-in-law.

In February 1978 Dick took Sharon along to Toy Fair. Ordinarily this was an exercise in goodwill for Dick and other reps. They would entertain customers and keep up on the new products. On the two previous occasions he had attended Toy Fair as a rep, Dick had written almost no business; he simply didn't have time. But this time, with Sharon along, they were able to give more individual attention to customers who were attending, and when the 12-day convention was over Dick and Sharon had orders on the books worth $4,000 in commissions. This not only paid for the trip but also bought new dining room furniture for their house.

A month after Toy Fair, Dick and his brother-in-law contracted for four booths at the toy show in Los Angeles. Several of their mutual principals chipped in and paid for the booth rental and sent their sales managers to help work the booths. As a result of this show, the pair wrote approximately $80,000 worth of business, bringing each about $4,000 in commissions—well worth their time and expense.

Shortly after returning from Los Angeles, Dick realized he was driving himself too hard. He was traveling almost constantly. Even though Sharon handled most of the paperwork as well as phone contact with customers, the job was becoming too much. Some of his customers commented on his extensive schedule and cautioned him to slow down.

One of Dick's most grueling trips was the one he made to Denver. He would leave at 4:00 A.M. Sunday morning so that he could arrive in Denver that evening. Then he would work every day through the following Saturday and arrive back home Sunday evening. His days were filled with selling chores, but he could usually see only one customer each day because of the details that had to be covered. He was not only working too hard, he wasn't even working smart. He simply couldn't visit all the customers he needed to call on.

It appeared that 1978 would bring in over $100,000 in commissions, and Dick decided that enough was enough. He set about hiring a salesman who would live in the Denver area and service Denver and the surrounding territory. This move would not only take a lot of pressure off Dick, but it would also mean better coverage and more sales in Colorado for him and his principals.

Above all, he wanted someone who was honest and willing to work hard. Familiarity with the toy and game industry he did not necessarily consider a prerequisite. Instead he felt that he could train someone in his successful mode of doing business and then wouldn't have to put up with preconceived notions of how the business should be run.

A toy-store owner in Colorado Springs, a friend of Dick's, had a 28-year-old son-in-law in the insurance business back east who was interested in moving west and was looking for a business opportunity. When Dick heard about this, he interviewed his friend's son-in-law and offered the young man a job—on straight commission—to cover Colorado and Wyoming.

The young man started with Dick August 1, 1978, and within six months was doing double the business Dick had expected at that point. Dick still makes an occasional trip to the Denver area to see old customers and confer with his new salesman.

A few months later Dick added a salesman in Salt Lake City, which cut down on his travel even more.

It's apparent that in a few short years Dick Cole has been able to take his business from ground zero to a very successful agency with a very attractive future. With no previous background as a rep or working for a rep agency, his achievement is even more amazing. However, through his ability to conceive new approaches to the rep–principal relationship, such as sending an order along with his contract acceptance, Dick has established himself as one of the leading manufacturers' representatives in the Rocky Mountain states.

ANALYSIS

If anyone was ever ripe for the rep business, it was Dick Cole. He had friends in the toy and game business all over the mountain states—people he had done favors for during the 15 years he worked for his game-company employer, people who were anxious to repay these favors by awarding him orders for good-quality products.

He also had a territory whose potential was unrecognized by many manufacturers who, consequently, did little or no business there. It was, therefore, not difficult for him to obtain lines.

His years of experience with one of the largest and most prestigious game manufacturers in the country gave him status that few reps could equal and made a real impression on prospective principals.

Sharon, his wife, had an intense interest in his success and was willing to devote her time to helping in the business. She actually recruited several lines for him, in addition to maintaining phone and mail contact with his customers. For Dick Cole, *not* to have become a manufacturers' representative would have been one of the biggest mistakes of his life.

Not all of us can do all of the things that make Dick Cole a success, but we can learn from his techniques.

Cultivate your customers while working as a direct employee. This applies not only to sales people but to anyone who has contact with the customers of his firm—engineers, management people, and even purchasing agents. Naturally salesmen and sales managers have the best opportunities. Anything you can do over the years to help your customers will be remembered when you hang out your own shingle. And don't hesitate to call on those customers when *you* need a favor.

Learning to negotiate commissions can be another plus. If the principal realizes that you can do a better job than its other reps, or if your territory requires extensive traveling, the principal may be willing to adjust the commission rate for your agency.

If you are approached by a principal that sells off-the-shelf items, try to send along an order or two when you return the signed contract.

Like Paul Elkin, whose story follows, Dick raised his working capital *before* entering the rep business. In his case it was providential—but it was also cash, and that's what matters. When things got tight, Dick could call on his banker and borrow a few thousand dollars to tide him over because he had established top credit in his past dealings with the money people.

The real lesson to be learned is that if you have a set of circumstances similar to Dick Cole's, with everything to gain by striking out on your own, don't waste any time. Jump in while the opportunity is there; it may never come back again.

4
PAUL ELKIN
A California
Entrepreneur

IN THE SPRING of 1975 Paul Elkin and I were driving through the Texas countryside enjoying the scenery and each other's company. At that time Paul was sales manager for one of our West Coast principals. The talk, as it often does with sales managers, turned into a discussion about the lifestyle of a manufacturers' representative: the good life, the income to be made—and the negatives: uncertainty, unresponsive principals, and extensive traveling.

As we neared Austin, Paul expressed a wish I had heard many times before. "I'd really like to be a manufacturers' representative," he said. I replied with the usual question, "Well, why not?" He responded, "Because I don't have $50,000," ending our conversation on that subject.

I thought no more about it. A rep agency is a common goal among many sales managers, and I'd had discussions of this type in the past. Usually it's mostly a fantasy for them, providing a Walter

[43]

Mitty sublimation and relief from the everyday pressures of a sales manager's job.

Paul, however, was an excellent sales manager, described as a professional by his successor at my principal's plant. I should have taken him more seriously, but his resigned air and comment about the $50,000 made me think there was little chance he would risk going out on his own.

On January 12, 1976, at 48 years of age Paul opened his agency, Paul M. Elkin Company, in Fullerton, California, and he didn't have $50,000. But he did have five lines and was on his way. I couldn't have been more surprised.

Paul was born and raised in The Bronx, the other end of the country from his eventual place of business. After graduating from high school, he spent a year in the armed services and was discharged in 1947. He went to Sampson College for two years and finished his degree at the University of Bridgeport at Bridgeport, Connecticut. With a major in business administration, Paul didn't have the faintest idea how he would put this degree to work. He recalls envying his peers who knew exactly what they wanted to do with their education. During the last semester at Bridgeport he married his wife, Estelle, a bilingual secretary at Lever Brothers in New York City.

Paul's great dream at that time was to move to California. He'd visited relatives there after leaving the service and liked the climate. Both he and his wife disliked the congestion and weather in the East. In the late forties California promised a warm climate and more breathing room. (It's still warm in Los Angeles, but no one moves there to escape traffic jams anymore.)

Practically broke after graduation, Paul went to work as an inspector for the Underwood Corporation to try to save enough money for his westward migration. Estelle also continued to work.

In 1952, when Paul was 24, he and Estelle left Connecticut for California. They stopped in Colorado Springs to visit Paul's brother-in-law's family. They had a wonderful visit, tarried a bit too long, and ran out of money in the process. So their trip was interrupted for a while—"ten years and three children," as Paul puts it.

Estelle was the first to find a job; she went to work for a fractional horsepower motor manufacturer as a secretary. Paul tried selling insurance, but found it wasn't right for him. He then went to work for the same company Estelle worked for, starting in the shipping and receiving department. Within a year, having worked through the stores department, material control, and production control, he finally became a buyer.

For two years he purchased a variety of commodities for his company, including powdered metal parts. During that time with the motor company, Paul noticed that certain off-the-shelf items—drills, taps, steel, and other basic raw materials—sometimes had to be bought from eastern sources. This was difficult because there were no local contacts for these commodities. He briefly considered the possibility that a manufacturers' representative could do very well representing some of these lines since such representation would fill an obvious need. "But I simply wasn't ready," Paul said. He pointed out that he was in his middle twenties at the time, and entry into the ranks of the self-employed was just too big a psychological step. That factor, plus only a fringe knowledge of the field and a definite lack of financial resources, kept Paul from seriously considering such a move. But the seed was planted.

After he had been with the company two years, business tailed off and people were reassigned to different positions. Sensing an unsettled period ahead and having gained an interest in the powdered metal process, Paul approached the general manager of the powdered metal company from which he had been purchasing parts. It was a small company and needed a sales manager; so after a couple of interviews Paul was hired.

In a small company such as Paul's new employer, the sales manager has to wear several hats. He must be very familiar with the technical end of the business in addition to his selling responsibilities. To accomplish this, Paul started with his new firm as foreman on the second shift. There he mixed the powder, ran the presses, operated the furnaces, and set up the tools. He did double duty, coming in during the day to handle his office work. The powdered metal process, which makes metal parts from metal powder, was just beginning to be appreciated by manufacturers, and Paul was fortunate in learning skills in an emerging industry. Since he had no technical background, this represented a real challenge to him. It seemed to come easy, however, and he soon had a thorough grasp of this complicated new process.

Paul increased his income handsomely, from $225 to $350 a month, when he began work at the powdered metal company. Estelle stopped working and they had their first child.

Eventually business improved and the company grew, allowing Paul the opportunity to concentrate almost completely on sales. As the company's horizons expanded, Paul saw the need for investigating markets outside the immediate Colorado area. He appointed manufacturers' representatives in Missouri, Minnesota, and Chicago. The Chicago rep was the late Paul Christman, former star quarterback for the old Chicago Cardinals and a great color-announcer for professional football telecasts.

In 1962 at the age of 35, Paul sat down and realistically analyzed his prospects for the future. He recognized that his community, Colorado Springs, would never be a highly industrialized area and that this would ultimately limit his ability to make a substantial living. With a wife and three children, Paul's income, while good for those days, permitted him little opportunity to save. Also, Paul and Estelle were very interested in the study of foreign cultures, and Colorado obviously offered very little opportunity for the pursuit of the hobby.

Consequently, in 1962 Paul decided to resume his interrupted trip to California. He contacted a powdered metal house in Los Angeles and, after suitable negotiations, was offered a position as sales engineer under the supervision of the sales manager. Sales engineers in this emerging technology were in short supply, and Paul went to work with a substantial increase in salary. His monthly income was now $815, plus a bonus based on sales volume in his assigned territory.

Paul progressed satisfactorily and enjoyed his job and the Los Angeles area. He purchased his present home in Fullerton and led a pleasant life. No particular thoughts about being a rep entered his head during this period other than the occasional fantasy that most salesmen have—a daydream about the nice life and large income available to the independent commissioned salesman.

In 1969 Paul's sales manager became ill and was out of the office for over six months. As the only other salesperson, Paul took on all sales obligations, turning his 8 A.M. to 5 P.M. job into a night and day affair. With his usual vigor he attacked the chore, and sales not only held their own but increased during this period. Eventually, however, the pace began to wear on him. With little relief in sight and only a modest increase in his paycheck, Paul became discouraged. After seven years with this company, at the age of 43, he answered a newspaper ad for a metallurgist for sales work in 11 western states. Over 100 replies were received by the eastern conglomerate that had placed the ad.

Paul was definitely not a metallurgist, but he knew that few metallurgists would answer an ad for sales work. He reasoned that his background in the powdered metal industry, which requires a working knowledge of metallurgy, made him a logical candidate for the job. He was right. The company hired him to sell its sophisticated products to the western aerospace and nuclear industry. His monthly income jumped from $1,050 to $1,460, an attractive increase and one guaranteed to eliminate any thoughts of starting a sales agency that might have been lurking in a wayward corner of his mind.

The job, however, turned out to be closely related in function to that of a manufacturers' representative. Paul worked from his home and had an answering service. With no immediate boss in the area, he set his own schedules and travel plans. His compensation and expenses were taken care of by the company, which, of course, was not a typical situation for a rep. Nevertheless, Paul feels this job was excellent training for what turned out to be his future career as a rep for one important reason: it taught him the art of self-discipline. Receiving little or no day-to-day direction from his superiors in the East, he was forced to get out of bed Monday mornings and do it all on his own. This is really the proof of the pudding, and Paul proved to himself that if the chance came along to start his own agency, self-discipline would not be one of his problems.

Nine months after taking this exciting job, Paul's career progress came to a screeching halt. The aerospace industry was the culprit. Government contracts were running out and Congress, arguing with the Pentagon about the direction of our military programs, was in no mood to vote additional millions. Thus the great "California shake-out" in aerospace began. Thousands of workers, engineers, and sales people lost their jobs in 1970. Paul Elkin was among them. In spite of his philosophy that lean times should mean increased sales efforts, Paul's employer back east didn't solicit his advice on management practices, and he received his notice.

Paul didn't escape the trauma that comes with the loss of a job. He had never before faced the prospect of not having a job, and his reaction was typical of anyone who has experienced such a shock. Fortunately, while he was adjusting to the situation, Estelle was able to find employment, and the family's income was not completely stopped.

While many former aerospace employees remained unemployed for months—in the case of highly specialized engineers, even years—Paul was able to find a job within 30 days. Again his 14 years of practical experience in the powdered metal industry proved invaluable. Not many unemployed salesmen had Paul's knowledge of this technical industry, and in January 1971 he began work at another Los Angeles firm at about the same salary he had been making when he lost his prior job.

Paul shared duties as sales manager with another salesman, each having responsibility for different industry groups. Theirs was an amiable relationship, and Paul was again enjoying his work and his lifestyle. But he really wanted more. By now he had a wealth of technical knowledge and a great flair for sales. These two traits, which are not often found in the same person, provide an ideal combination for a manufacturers' representative.

At this time he became more and more determined to start his own sales agency. He knew that at the age of 48, this was a tricky prospect. If his agency failed, it would be harder to find another job. However, since his three children were now virtually self-supporting and Estelle had continued to work, Paul felt the risk would be worth the potential goodies—independence and the possibility of a significantly better income. So he began to plan, and plan thoroughly, for his own agency.

Paul wanted to choose his lines carefully so that he would have a minimum of competition. Most of his career had been spent selling goods not available from the majority of salesmen in the field. For example, there are eight or ten plants making metal stampings for every one making powdered metal parts. Specialty lines *are* specialty lines because they require highly technical sales skills and manufacturing expertise. Paul felt he had this capability and decided if he couldn't obtain these types of lines at first, he would wait until they became available to begin his agency.

In the fall of 1975 Paul began to write selected firms that he thought would meet his requirements. Gradually he started receiving replies to letters he had mailed to specialty manufacturers, most of them either indicating they weren't interested at present or that they already had representation in the area. However, there were some replies that showed interest in what Paul had to offer. Although they were few in number, he was pleased. As a salesman, he knew that success in selling can be achieved with a small percentage of yes answers, and he had received that percentage.

Signing them up, however, was another story. Paul was gainfully employed as a salesman, and there was no question about his ability to sell. But his ability to manage his own sales agency was unknown. Perhaps the major turning point came when his former powdered-metal-company employer in Colorado Springs showed its confidence in him by offering him its line. It allowed him to choose his own timing so that he could pick the most opportune date to begin his agency. With this knowledge firmly in mind, Paul became more serious about reaching a final commitment with some of the other companies he had contacted. Another firm making a specialty metal part also showed interest and a few weeks later gave him a contract.

Still another company making specialized castings was contacted by Paul, and the firm's owners said they would be interested in working with him because his other products were quite compatible with the casting line.

While Paul was still employed, an executive of an eastern firm came to visit and discuss a part that Paul's company was making for a mutual customer. An assembly was involved, and the two companies had to work together to be certain that the parts from both firms would be compatible.

At lunch the discussion turned to sales philosophies, and Paul mentioned that he was thinking of becoming a manufacturers' representative. The visiting executive, having worked with Paul over a period of time, obviously liked what he saw and told Paul to contact him as soon as he established his agency. Without hesitation, the executive said he wanted Paul to represent his company on the West Coast.

Not all contacts were initiated by Paul. A friend of his, a midwestern executive, was asked by the sales manager of one of his customers if he knew of anyone on the West Coast he could recommend as a rep for the firm. Paul's friend knew of his plans to start his own agency. Moreover he had worked with Paul and was aware of his sales expertise and technical ability. He recommended Paul, and the sales manager signed him up. The company had some business in Paul's territory and had proved that it could compete there even though its facilities were back east.

Paul was getting closer to the time when he would be leaving his company, but he had some very important plans that had to be carried out prior to his departure.

His first concern was start-up capital—the name of the game. He had a few lines with existing business that would bring him a modest income from the beginning, perhaps $200 to $300 a month, but this would cover only a small portion of his projected business and living expenses. During the last few years Paul had made an effort to put a few dollars into savings each month and now had a modest sum sitting in his local bank, but it was not enough to carry him for long.

He still lived in the house he bought when he moved to California in 1962. His mortgage had been reduced by a considerable amount, and he was able to refinance it. He owed approximately $13,000 on his $30,000 mortgage; so he was able to realize about $17,000 in cash for his business. He also purchased a new car for use in his business. He refinanced the house and purchased the car *while still employed,* a very intelligent move. Estelle was still working, but Paul was determined to build his business as quickly as possible to the point where it would be the sole support of his family.

The time had arrived. Paul had raised his start-up capital and had five companies ready to go with him. He gave notice at his firm. With his five lines he was in business from the very beginning. His first concern was to find an office, and he located a convenient office complex just a short distance from his home. He made his requirements known to the leasing company, which put him in touch with a tenant who had a spare office, completely furnished, available for $75 a month.

Paul had worked on the West Coast for 14 years and during that period had become acquainted with purchasing and engineering personnel at many prominent industrial concerns. Moreover, these same companies were usually excellent prospects for the products of the companies he now represented. So he set about making calls throughout his entire territory. This included not only the Los Angeles area but Northern California, Arizona, and Nevada.

While it's easy and important to visit acquaintances in the field, it's also important to visit new prospective customers; so Paul mixed it up and saw numerous potential users of his companies' products.

None of his former customers had known that Paul was going to enter the rep business, and they were surprised to learn of his new venture. His card, which named the product lines he represented, could be placed by his business friends and acquaintances in their files for reference whenever a particular need arose.

Calls on former customers also resulted in his obtaining another excellent line. A chief engineer pointed out to Paul that one of his company's products would be less salable in the future since it was being replaced by a newer and less expensive component being made by a Dallas company. Paul got in touch with the sales manager of the Texas firm and was told that the company had just terminated its West Coast agency. This alarmed Paul, since the word *termination* isn't a rep's favorite expression. However, the sales manager related a sad tale of three years of falling sales in a rapidly rising market for his product. He also added another bit of information that convinced Paul his company was a good one. The terminated rep had been with the company for 20 years, and the most recent addition to the firm's rep force had been 18 years earlier. Recognizing the stability of the company, Paul signed on another very fine principal.

Finances were improving. Paul soon moved into his own office in the same complex at $105 a month. Some small commissions were coming in, but his powdered metal house had, for a limited time, agreed to only 2½ percent commission—instead of the customary 5 percent—on existing business in the area. Its contribution was therefore helpful but not startling. He would, of course, receive 5 percent on all new business he brought in. Another principal was giving him a full 5 percent on existing business, but this amounted to only $100 to $200 a month. His casting company helped considerably by giving him a $300 draw against the commissions he would earn.

As the first year went on, Paul's efforts started to pay off and commissions began to grow. He was also able to renegotiate his arrangement with his powdered metal company, bringing commissions up to a full 5 percent on existing business. Still, custom-engineered products, which made up the bulk of his lines, take time to develop. The rep is often in on a new product from the time it is only a gleam in a design engineer's eye until it becomes a full-fledged product. This can take months and often years. Not infrequently the entire project is shelved somewhere along the line.

Nevertheless, by the end of 1976 Paul's gross commissions came to $10,000—commendable earnings for a rep's first year but nowhere near the income Paul needed.

Paul's records showed that his expenses ran approximately $1,250 per month, or about $15,000 a year. This figure represented expenses only and included no personal income. Still, he had an excellent start. He was also pleased that he had several projects on the fire that would be coming through in 1977, his second year in business. Because he had performed so well for his casting firm, a local establishment, it renegotiated his contract and put him in charge of all sales. While his commission percentage was reduced and his draw eliminated, the larger volume brought him more actual income.

During his first year in business, Paul was conscientious about making regular calls on both current and prospective customers. He felt these buyers and engineers should know that he was in business for real. Without regular visits, they might have some reason to doubt his ability to stay in business and service their accounts effectively. Too many new reps make one visit to a potential customer and are never seen again.

Professional buyers and engineers are accustomed to the "one-time Charlie" and usually want to see repeated visits by a new rep before entering into serious negotiations. During his follow-up visits Paul dropped off ball-point pens inscribed with his company name. While this is not a particularly innovative idea, it kept his name in front of prospective buyers, again assuring them he was in business.

During his second year Paul and his casting principal again renegotiated their contract. Paul relinquished responsibility for all the company's sales and reverted to a straight 5 percent commission on accounts he had obtained for the firm. This didn't appreciably affect his overall revenue, but by December 1977, the end of his second year in business, his annual gross income had increased to $28,000—an excellent performance for a two-year man. Not only was Paul able to meet his expenses, but he had funds left over for himself. His living costs, just like everyone else's, had increased; he had a higher mortgage payment and was thinking about buying a new car.

Succeeding as he did during the first two years encouraged Paul considerably. He continued working hard, but he was careful to pace himself. Because of his wife's income and his determination not to lose sight of the fact that life should be lived to the fullest, he and Estelle took a three-week trip to Japan. These trips to foreign countries have become a custom of long standing for the Elkins. They enjoy studying and participating in foreign cultures and have traveled extensively.

The culmination of Paul's planning and hard work came when he added up the gross commissions of his agency at the end of 1978. He was extremely pleased to find that he had grossed enough not only to pay his business and living expenses and Uncle Sam, but to have something left for savings and investment.

When asked about his general view of the rep business, as a three-year veteran, Paul made two points. "First," he said, "being a rep can be one of the most rewarding and satisfying lifestyles I can imagine. However, it can also be terribly frustrating. As a sales manager of a company, you're usually involved with one product line, and this keeps things fairly simple. When things go wrong you can go to the production manager and do a little desk pounding. In other words, you have the authority to do something about a problem whether it be a noncompetitive pricing structure or a late delivery of product.

"This same luxury isn't available to the rep. When his customers start complaining to him about deficiencies at his principals' plants, he must approach the principals' sales managers and diplomatically request corrective action. Frequently this isn't prompt in arriving. Because he doesn't have any authority with the company, the rep's requests often go unanswered. This reduces his ability to be effective and places all his lines in jeopardy with disenchanted customers. Fortunately, principals are becoming more aware of the services reps provide and are consequently becoming responsive to their requests.

"Second, by being independent I can take advantage of opportunities that would have to be passed by if I worked as a salaried employee. If some venture or investment looks promising, I don't have to request the afternoon off to investigate its possibilities. As a rule, I can attend to it then and there.

"Naturally my principals come first and, until I add sales personnel, I can't be completely free to pursue certain opportunities that would consume a great deal of time. Still, there are plenty of chances to work on projects without penalizing my working time appreciably."

Paul will no doubt continue to be successful. He has set some very definite goals for himself, outlining where he wants to be in five years and in ten years. There's no doubt in my mind about his ability to reach those goals.

ANALYSIS

To meet Paul Elkin casually would leave you with the impression that he fits the mold of a good salesman and sales manager. But to work with him, as I have, is to know the other side of Paul.

When he was my sales manager, I noticed that on each visit to a customer he would whip out his ever present yellow pad and make detailed notes about the call—what the customer requested, when he wanted it, and why he wanted it. Back in his Los Angeles office, Paul would give immediate priority to these requests and then we would have happy customers all over Texas.

This penchant for detail and follow-up, in addition to his sales and technical talents, explains why Paul Elkin got off to a happy beginning. He didn't have the $50,000 he had thought necessary for survival—though he does wonder how he made it on his savings and refinancing funds—but he was perceptive enough to not make the break from steady employment until most of the machinery was in place and oiled up.

He arranged for the refinancing of his mortgage and the purchase of a car *before* becoming a rep, knowing this would be almost impossible once he left work and had no paychecks to offer as evidence of his ability to repay these debts. Again—before starting out—he lined up good, solid principals, thereby assuring himself a welcome reception at the companies that would turn out to be his best customers. He conquered the desire to start on his own until all his self-determined requirements were met. Then, and only then, did he cut the cord.

Not all prospective reps will have Paul's patience with detail and his thoroughness, but these are traits to be emulated as much as possible. It means a postponement in getting started, but a few months' delay—or even a year or two on the front end—can mean a much happier existence when you do begin your venture.

Paul's courage to take this step at the age of 48 is proof that the combination of experience and maturity goes a long way toward helping you get off to a running start. Going over breakeven in his second year was exceptional, and these two things contributed greatly toward his quick success.

If you are not a young man but have used the years to absorb knowledge about your field and make friends and acquaintances in your potential customer group, take heart from Paul Elkin—it's never too late to start.

5
PAUL MITCHELL
Building Materials Specialist

IT'S RARE TO find a businessman who works in the same community he was born in. During the last few decades our mobile society has transplanted millions of families, so it was a pleasant surprise to find that Paul Mitchell, a Canton, Massachusetts, manufacturers' rep, is a native of the Boston area and has spent his entire business life in this New England community.

At 39 Paul still has a long way to go before claiming he has spent his entire life in New England, but the odds are very much in favor of his being able to make this claim upon retirement some 30 years or more from now. Reps almost never leave the area in which they built their business. Their whole future is tied to the customer relationships they develop over the years; to throw these over and start up elsewhere is to throw away assets of inestimable value.

After graduating from high school, Paul got a job with a local branch of a major chain in the building materials business. He began in the retail sales end of the company and learned the business from the ground up. His intent was not necessarily to stay in lumber and building materials but to keep himself alive and pay his way through Northeastern University. After graduation he could decide what vocation to follow. Among his choices, of course, was the building materials business.

Paul worked a five-day week plus two evenings. In addition, he attended Northeastern on two of his free evenings. This was a tremendous grind and hard on his constitution. About a year after starting with the firm, he was transferred to the contractor sales division of the company, where he sold building materials to builders and contractors. This required outside selling and involved Paul in considerable activity, so much so that he decided to take a break from school.

In the contractor sales end of the business, Paul was again working mostly as a salesman. However, on certain large sales where competition was keen, he became involved in some purchasing functions and gained knowledge about the procurement end of the business. During the time he spent with the firm, he received a well-rounded background in the building materials industry.

After about five years with this chain, Paul was offered a sales position with a New Jersey firm. His territory was the general Boston area, which at that time was bringing in a gross volume of about $225,000. So in 1966 at the age of 25, he accepted the new job at a salary of $10,000 a year. Within five years he had increased sales in his area to $1.2 million. Even though he was able to accomplish this remarkable increase in sales, his maximum yearly income was held to around $22,000 through the application of quotas by his employer. One year his quota was increased by $300,000 and later he was given a $600,000 increase. Since total income was governed by a salesman's ability to reach his quota, it was easy for the company to use this system to control the earnings of its sales people.

In Paul's case the constant increases in quotas acted as a demotivating force, and he found himself working just hard enough to reach whatever sales figure the company applied to him. He started taking longer lunch breaks and spending an occasional weekday afternoon on the golf course. He realized this wasn't the way he wanted to spend the rest of his life. He didn't dislike his job, but he grew bored with it because of the lack of incentive and opportunity.

He had been offered positions with the company in other areas, but Paul had strong roots in Boston and wasn't interested in moving. He also felt there would be no significant advantage in moving, because the company's overall remuneration policy seemed aimed at keeping wages within certain parameters, regardless of the performance of the individual salesman.

At the age of 30 Paul took a good long look at what the future would bring. After appraising his opportunities with his present firm as dismal, he began to consider other career options.

During his years in sales work, Paul had had many opportunities to meet and visit with other salesmen while waiting to see buyers at his customers' offices. He had noticed that one particular breed of salesman—the manufacturers' representative—seemed a bit more successful and independent than the company salesmen he knew. They also drove bigger cars, were better dressed, and gave every appearance of making excellent incomes. Paul admits to being Irish and says the Irish trait of talking to anyone who will listen was a big help to him in finding out how these reps worked. Many of them explained to him the role of the rep—how they got started and the promising future that was opening up as firms over the country increasingly took advantage of this form of selling.

Paul also had a good friend who had been in the agency business for about 18 years and who was doing very well. He had lunch with this friend several times and visited the agency office to determine whether he should consider trying the rep business. His friend was very helpful, and in the course of their discussions suggested that Paul come to work for him. This agency owner had the foresight to plan for his firm's continuity. Together, he and Paul agreed that after two years they would review their compatibility and the overall results with the possibility of Paul's gradually acquiring ownership of the agency.

When Paul went into his employer's office and offered his resignation, he mentioned that he was going into the agency business.

His employer pointed out that this was a very risky business and added that his firm used agents only to open up new territories, after which the reps were replaced by direct-employee salesmen. In addition, he offered Paul a $7,000 annual increase to remain with the company.

Realizing that he had been underpaid for several years and disgusted by the company's treatment of its reps, Paul was even more determined to leave and he did so on the spot. This experience made him more resolute than ever about giving the agency business a good hard try.

When he started with the agency, Paul was given a territory then producing about $12,000 a year in commissions. His beginning draw was based on this figure. This was of little concern to Paul since his previous selling experience had given him tremendous self-confidence in his ability to sell, regardless of the product. This confidence was all the more amazing because the agency's product lines consisted of power equipment—lawn mowers, tillers, and major construction machinery—a radical departure from the products he had been selling for the past ten years.

After a short indoctrination in the ways of power tools, Paul set out calling on power equipment distribution companies and small rental yards. He was still confident of his selling ability, but he nevertheless discovered that some mechanical know-how would have made his job much easier. Customers wanted to know the whys and wherefores of engines and hydraulics. Although he picked up some of this knowledge as he went along, he still felt he would have sold more in a shorter time had he been more mechanically inclined.

Paul's sales volume increased at a good but not spectacular rate. By the end of his second year with the agency, his share of commissions was approximately $18,000—or a 50 percent increase over his starting income.

In the second year he began to reflect on whether or not his future was with the agency. Two considerations troubled him. First, he wasn't sure that he really liked selling power equipment even though he was beginning to feel more comfortable with it. He realized that he missed selling building materials, which had long ago become second nature to him. Second, he wasn't sure whether in the long run he would be happy working for someone else. His two-year stint as an agency employee made him long to have his own rep business and be in complete control.

So after thinking long and hard about his options, he sat down with the agency owner and told him that at the end of that year he would like to leave the agency and return to selling building materials—his real love—as an independent manufacturers' representative. Paul's employer understood his strong desire to have his own business and wished him well.

It was now time to seek out good companies to represent. Paul immediately thought of a firm whose products he had previously sold when working with the building materials firm. He phoned the company's vice-president of sales and asked if he could be considered as a commissioned representative for the firm in New England. The sales executive was reluctant to simply award the line to Paul and suggested that they meet for further discussions. The two men met six or seven times and talked for over 20 hours before coming to an agreement. The vice-president was naturally concerned about Paul's familiarity with the rep field and questioned his ability to stay in business. Paul countered by explaining that he had purposely spent two years working for a sales agency in order to learn the ropes and was certain he would succeed.

He finally convinced the vice-president that he could do the job and was awarded the line. It was not a tremendous break, since the company had little business in Paul's area, but it did mean that he was established in the business and had a line to prove it. He pursued another line in a similar manner and started his agency in April 1973 with two lines and a lot of enthusiasm.

When Paul decided to go on his own, he had a financing plan in mind that he thought was practical and sufficient. Over the years he had managed to accumulate approximately $12,000 in securities, which he now cashed in. He also had a very understanding banker and was therefore able to borrow $8,000. This gave him a total of $20,000 to start his business and feed his family.

Paul's early efforts were concentrated on financing and other details relative to start-up. He finally woke up one morning and realized he was attempting to launch a rep business with only two lines. While these lines were good ones, even with maximum effort they could never bring in enough commissions to make his agency successful. Consequently, for the next six months he spent more time finding lines than he did selling.

His solicitation of additional lines was rather unusual. He approached several firms he was selling to, and had sold to in his previous jobs, and asked if they would help him out. He told his buying and executive acquaintances at these firms that he was going after certain lines and asked their aid in giving him good solid references. In all cases he was told to go ahead. Thus he was able to approach the principals he had in mind with the blessings of his future customers for those particular lines. When the principals phoned for references, Paul was assured they would be pleased with the responses they received. He signed up several firms with this technique.

In one or two instances his friends took things into their own hands and phoned companies directly, suggesting that Paul would be an exceptionally fine representative for their lines.

Despite his concentration on securing prospective principals, Paul was able to do some selling, and at the end of nine months he had received commissions totaling just under $9,000, or a little less than $1,000 a month. Although this would be considered a better-than-average beginning for many reps, it didn't satisfy Paul. He had used a sizable amount of his capital in running his business and supporting his family, and his funds were running low. Fortunately, a close relative came to his rescue and provided another loan of $8,000, to be paid off at the same rate as his bank loan for the same amount. While this was a welcome addition to his working capital, it increased his monthly loan payments.

At the beginning of his second year, however, Paul shifted into third gear and really began working hard. He estimates that his average workweek was 60 hours. This was supplemented by another 40 hours that his wife, Loretta, spent helping him with office detail and bookwork.

One thing often overlooked by a new rep is the amount of paperwork involved in running a sales agency. With eight or nine principals flooding you with copies of order acknowledgments, shipping notices, invoices, and correspondence, merely keeping the files orderly and effective can require 10 to 15 hours a week. Add to this the normal office routine—phone calls, purchasing supplies, and a tremendous amount of bookkeeping—and you can easily fall behind unless you have additional help. Loretta was typical of many reps' wives; she pitched in and made it possible for Paul to focus his energies on selling—which is, of course, the prime duty of a one-man-agency owner. Even today Loretta works about 20 hours a week but now has the help of a part-time employee every day.

At the end of his second year Paul's total commissions were $26,000, quite a handsome increase. But his business expenses didn't diminish; instead they increased. He estimates that only about $14,000 of this income was used for personal living expenses. Contrast this with the $18,000 he received for his last year at his friend's agency, all of which could be used for family support, and you can understand Paul's feeling that he wasn't progressing very rapidly.

Actually, of course, he was doing exceptionally well for a second-year man; but with no significant means of comparison available, except for his previous income, he became somewhat discouraged. One of the factors contributing to Paul's discouragement was the rather seasonal aspect of most of his lines. He would have two or three excellent months followed by several poor months. Although this was a natural consequence of the type of lines he was carrying, it was nevertheless disturbing.

Rather than attempt to find lines that would be good for the entire year, Paul discovered a much more practical remedy. He sought out principals whose products could be sold effectively in what he knew to be poor months for his present lines. While this took longer than finding year-round lines, it worked out well in the end. He kept his current lines that were selling well and didn't have to introduce all new lines to his customers.

His hard work started to pay off in 1975. With lines that he could enthusiastically sell most of the year, Paul felt his turnaround year was at hand, and it was. By the end of that year his agency's commissions were approximately $40,000. He had also paid off his loans and no longer had any indebtedness. Now he could keep a larger share of the proceeds for himself and look ahead to a prosperous future. His hunch was correct, and 1976 proved to be another banner year with commissions increasing again.

Paul had finally made it. His agency was prospering and his financial future, barring some unforeseen event, seemed assured. What more could a person ask? To Paul, there was something more he could ask—a little free time. He was still putting in 60 hours a week. He hadn't taken a vacation since he started the business, because when he wasn't there, nothing happened. He was even hesitant to take a day off for fear a big order would be missed or a principal would be miffed at not being able to reach him. This was not entirely realistic, but when you work so hard to nurture your own business into a successful entity, it's normal to lose some perspective.

Paul was enjoying his business but not his life. He had a talk with himself and decided that working is only part of a man's obligation. He also owes his family and himself time to enjoy the fruits of his labor. Not one to tarry long about making decisions, he began to make plans to enlarge his agency. Not only would this allow him free time, it would result in a business organization that could accomplish much more than a one-man agency and also be worth something to him financially in later years.

In the summer of 1976 Paul started looking for a capable salesman to add to his agency. He knew many sales people among his business acquaintances and talked to several of them to determine whether they would be likely candidates for the job. For one reason or another, none of them quite fitted the image Paul had in mind. Some weren't familiar enough with his type of products, and others couldn't quite comprehend the role of a salesman for a rep agency.

Paul didn't stop looking, but he slowed down his recruitment activities for several months.

On a Sunday in July 1977, one of his sales managers phoned him to chat. The call seemed to be more social than business, and Paul sensed that the sales manager had something on his mind other than next year's sales forecast. For that reason he asked, "Don, what's going on? Have you been fired?" Don replied, "No, Paul, but I'm thinking of leaving the company and becoming a rep. I've seen how well some of you fellows do and may want to strike out on my own. I thought I'd call you for a little helpful advice."

Paul, remembering how difficult it had been for him to reach his present stage, had concern for his friend's ambitions and said, "Don, come up to see me, and I'll be glad to tell you everything I know about the business—the good and the bad."

He realized that even though Don had worked with reps for years, he still knew about sales agencies only from a company viewpoint. Often knowing only one side of the business is not enough to insure the success of a new agency. In their phone conversation, Paul also mentioned to Don that he was thinking of enlarging his agency and that this might be an alternative to Don's original plans.

As a result of several visits both men decided that Paul's latter suggestion would be mutually beneficial. Don had lived in New England before and was familiar with the territory. He knew the product lines and was well acquainted with many of Paul's present and potential customers. So in September 1977, Paul Mitchell Associates became a two-man firm—incorporated under the name of Mitchell Associates, Inc.

With both men covering the New England area, sales improved considerably for the agency's principals. Before long Paul found himself again spending all day in the field and keeping up with office communications at night. In essence he had reached a new plateau and was again in need of additional help.

In the spring of 1978 Paul became interested in the talents of an acquaintance in the beauty aids business—a far cry from building materials. However, the man had been a professional salesman for over 20 years and, in Paul's words, "could sell flypaper to flies." The salesman was not happy with his employment situation, and after several visits Paul indicated to him that Mitchell Associates might be able to offer him a job in the fall.

In July this acquaintance called and said he had just left his job and was ready to go to work for Paul's agency. Paul was somewhat surprised—it was several months prior to their agreed-upon date—but he looked over his bank balance and decided that he could work out the financial end. Later in the month Mitchell Associates, Inc. became a three-man agency. Paul found, as he had suspected all along, that his new rep took quickly to the agency's lines and in a few months became a definite asset to the firm.

At this point Paul had a well-rounded group of lines in building materials—imitation brick, glazing compound, molding accessories, insulation products, and several other lines purchased by most wholesale building materials firms. He decided that because of the growing awareness of our country's energy requirements, the time had come to take on some energy-related lines. He added coal-burning fireplaces and glass fireplace enclosures to his group of lines and was able to sell them to most of his existing customers.

Paul's commissions range from 6 to 7½ percent, but occasionally he will negotiate a higher commission if the line is new to New England and a lot of missionary work is required. He is straightforward in his approach to his principals, which, he admits, has its good and bad points. But his philosophy is to have everything out on the table and, in this manner, eliminate most misunderstandings about product quality and commissions. Paul feels his directness may have cost him a line or two even before he obtained them, but he's very comfortable with his present principals and he believes there is a mutual feeling of openness, which makes for profitable relationships.

At 39 Paul is looking down the road toward further expansion of his agency, but he doesn't feel this is possible through his present lines. They will continue to grow, of course, but he thinks that a good base has been established for his principals, and the additional growth can be easily handled by his present complement of sales people.

He expects that the route to a larger agency—probably a five-man organization at most—will be through a separate group of principals not necessarily related to his present group. A diversification into automotive products or some similar industry that represents a departure from building materials is one of Paul's thoughts at this time. However, his line of thinking is just that at this point—a line of thinking. He has made no plans in this direction and probably won't until he loses that feeling of challenge that has always been the catalyst for his successful career moves.

ANALYSIS

Like Paul Rice, Paul Mitchell got his feet wet in this business by first working for another rep agency. The two years of experience he acquired in this manner made his entry into the field much easier than it would have been had he jumped in without any previous knowledge of how things work. He became familiar with the dollar figures necessary to keep an agency alive, learned how to negotiate for lines, and became schooled in the talents needed to run an agency. Therefore, he was well prepared to launch his own business. Naturally there were some surprises, but Paul did get to break-even day in a relatively short time.

His return to the building materials business was also a smart move. Perhaps he could have remained with the agency in the power equipment business, but he wouldn't have been happy selling those products. And, of course, he might never have started or owned his own agency. You can see from Paul's experience, as well as that of the other reps you've been reading about, that success in this business is more easily attained if you sell a product that you know something about. To start a rep business *and* learn a completely new product line is asking for trouble.

Paul, like Dick Cole, used his prior customer contacts to decided advantage when seeking quality principals. He made certain in advance that good references would be furnished by these business friends and acquaintances. This is a fine example to follow at any stage of agency development, but it's particularly beneficial when your agency is new or only a few months old. At that point manufacturers are understandably hesitant to put their eggs in your basket. They know not all reps will make the grade, and they are legitimately concerned about their own reputation if they appoint a rep who goes out of business in a few months. Having good strong customer references doesn't mean you can sign up every principal you go after, but it will sway the decision in your favor more often than not.

Paul also had the good sense to recognize that lifestyle is as important as money. Many reps, when their incomes start to increase handsomely, work harder and longer and enjoy life less, ultimately burdening themselves beyond their physical endurance. When Paul recognized some of these early symptoms, he didn't wait too long before adding personnel to his agency. And when the same threat appeared again, he added still another man. Not only did he then enjoy life more by spreading the work around, but he also fulfilled his obligation to his principals to continue improving the sales of their products.

Things look good for Paul Mitchell. He always stays a step ahead of whatever is happening, and I predict a long and successful future for his agency. If you try to keep looking ahead as Paul did, you too—if that is your aim—can develop a profitable multi-man sales agency.

6
DAN JURGENS
Registered Pharmacist (and Manufacturers' Representative)

IT WOULD BE an understatement to say that few registered pharmacists turn from pharmacology to the manufacturers' rep business. Dan Jurgens is the only one I've been able to turn up and, not surprisingly, his new career isn't a complete departure from the pharmaceutical field; the products he sells are related to the medical and scientific professions.

Dan Jurgens didn't become a pharmacist to work in a drugstore. He always knew that he wanted to be a salesman. With his interest in pharmacy, he felt the ideal career would be that of a detail man for one of the major drug companies, introducing new and improved drugs and medications to doctors.

Dan was born and raised in Pekin, Illinois, a small city about 150 miles south of Chicago. While in high school he worked part time in a drugstore where he developed much of his interest in the field of pharmacy.

In 1954 Dan left Pekin for Purdue University in neighboring Indiana and set out to earn his degree. He had every intention of becoming a drug detail man upon graduation and supplemented his course work by working one summer as a control chemist for a large chemical company in his hometown of Pekin.

During his last year at Purdue, he contacted several leading pharmaceutical houses and offered his services as a drug detail man, fully expecting that his degree would open the employment doors. Unfortunately, that was not the case.

Had colleges and universities been as sophisticated in 1958 as they are now in terms of graduate placement and career services, Dan would have quickly learned that an unmarried man in excellent physical condition with no previous military service was not an ideal candidate for employment, particularly by the large pharmaceutical houses. New employees required extensive training to successfully present products to the medical profession. Spending thousands of dollars training a young man only to have him whisked off to the Army or Navy was not one of their top priorities. They were looking for men less likely to leave them for Uncle Sam.

At this point Dan also learned, much to his surprise, that drug firms weren't enthusiastic about hiring pharmacists as detail men. They seemed to feel that too much knowledge was more a hindrance than a help. Drug detail men are thoroughly schooled by companies to say exactly what the companies want them to say about their drugs. In this manner, companies eliminate the danger of a detail man elaborating on a product's virtues to the point of possible misrepresentation. A trained pharmacist, with his background in chemistry, might be tempted to interpret certain qualities of a drug in a way that could cause a doctor to misunderstand its application. This in turn could lead to problems for the companies if doctors expected results that were not possible.

So after four years of hard work and study Dan found, as he neared graduation in the spring of 1958, that his employment possibilities were somewhat bleak and his goal of becoming a detail salesman was appearing less and less realistic.

Unknown to Dan, about that time the Summit, Illinois, plant of the Pekin chemical company he had worked for one summer was looking for a control chemist in its research department. The chief chemist in Pekin had been impressed with Dan's work and had kept track of him. Consequently, he suggested that the research department contact Dan to see if he was available. When Dan received the company's letter, he immediately went to Summit for an interview. After graduation he went to work for the firm as a control chemist.

Now located in the Chicago area, Dan became reacquainted with a high school classmate from Pekin, Norma Wolfer. They were married in March 1959.

Although his personal affairs were humming along to his satisfaction, the same couldn't be said about his business life. Being cooped up in a laboratory all day reinforced his conviction that he really wanted to be a salesman. He tired of the routine chores performed by a control chemist. An extrovert by nature, he missed the opportunity of meeting and getting to know new people.

Dan reached the point where he wondered occasionally if he could find a good reason to call in sick. Since he was in excellent health and had a conscience to deal with, he would wind up going to work, but dreading it.

It finally dawned on him that if he was looking for reasons not to show up for work, he was in pretty bad shape. To make matters worse, he resented the daily 70-mile round trip to his job from the house he had rented in Rolling Meadows, Illinois.

Norma finally made up his mind for him. "Look, Dan," she said, "if you really want to be a salesman, this is an excellent time to find out whether that's the career for you. I'm working, and there aren't any children to worry about, so go out and see if you can find a sales job that suits you."

At that time, about three years after Dan graduated from Purdue, he and Norma were together earning about $10,000 a year, a good but not spectacular income for 1961. Dan admits he was reticent about venturing into a new field where the income would be uncertain. However, since Norma was bringing in almost half of their income and he knew they wouldn't go broke if things didn't work out, he decided to give sales a try. With his strong desire to get into the field, he felt he had a better-than-even chance to succeed.

Dan was still interested in the possibility of using his pharmaceutical background, but he also realized that after working as a control chemist for four years he was exceptionally well acquainted with laboratory equipment. His experience in working with laboratory associates also gave him excellent insight into the types of products that would appeal to the scientists and chemists who populated the area's labs. After some thought he decided he would like to try selling lab supplies. This decision was his first step toward becoming a rep, although that event was still years down the road. At that time, had you asked him, Dan wouldn't have been able to tell you what a rep was, much less what he did.

His decision made, Dan obtained a job with a full-line laboratory-supply house that distributed the products of a number of companies and also manufactured some custom glassware. The custom glassware capabilities of the firm, coupled with Dan's naivete as a new salesman, brought in one of the company's best accounts.

A local university had extensive lab facilities and used an attractive volume of glassware as well as other supplies. Dan, however, had been warned by veteran salesmen not to bother with the account. They patiently explained that everything the school purchased was bought on a bid basis and that several larger firms consistently submitted exceptionally low bids at very marginal profit levels. Dan's company, interested in a fair profit, could not meet these bids.

Still young, full of enthusiasm, and admittedly naive, Dan thought he would give it a try anyhow. He soon realized that the veteran salesmen knew what they were talking about. The university did purchase by bid, and Dan's company couldn't be competitive. Still, he continued to distribute his catalog to anyone at the school wearing a smock, including some art students. He also gave one to a young assistant purchasing agent who, after several visits by Dan, became interested in the company's products, particularly its custom glassware capabilities.

Shortly thereafter Dan made a discovery that neutralized much of the advice passed on to him by the veteran sales people; he found that not *all* of the school's purchases were made on a bid basis. An order could be issued at the sole discretion of the purchasing department without a formal bid, provided the total amount didn't exceed $150.

The well-placed catalogs started to produce results. Requisitions were sent to the purchasing office for the products Dan's company distributed and also for custom glassware. The young purchasing man started placing orders with Dan, all under $150, but all at the standard price that included a good profit for the company. Ultimately, Dan was receiving as much business via small, individual purchase orders as were his competitors on the formal bid basis. But his business was much more profitable, and the university became one of his largest customers. This experience was a good lesson for Dan. He quickly learned to use his own judgment and common sense in selling instead of relying entirely on the advice of others.

Dan wasn't on a commission arrangement with his employer, but the more he sold, the more often he received increases in salary. By 1964 he was making approximately $8,000 a year and doing the kind of work he'd always dreamed about.

Still, Dan felt he needed an incentive and the opportunity to make more money based on his ability, so in June 1964 he went to work for a manufacturing company in a related field, but with only one product. Dan's starting salary was $10,000 a year.

He had been in his new job only eight months when the company changed its entire marketing philosophy and laid off most of its sales people, Dan included. Ironically, he had just purchased a new home in Carol Stream, Illinois; he had a big mortgage, a small baby, and his wife was not working. These added up to rather large obligations at just the wrong time. His income was about to stop, and he had no job. In Dan's own words, "It was panic time."

It turned out, however, that it wasn't "panic time" after all. Dan phoned the general manager of a manufacturing firm that had wanted to hire him when he was still with the laboratory-supply company but had not done so because of its policy of not hiring sales people away from its distributors. Since Dan hadn't worked for the distributor for several months, he was eligible for employment with the manufacturing firm, and the general manager created a job for him. Fortunately, or unfortunately, Dan went back to work without missing a paycheck.

The new job put him in the role of a goodwill man for his company. He would go out on minor service calls and for adjustments of the company's products in laboratories throughout the Midwest. These repairs and adjustments were made at no charge to the labs and created much goodwill for the firm. Of course Dan wouldn't leave a call without pointing out the attractive features of one or more of the company's other products. If a customer showed genuine interest in a product, Dan would arrange for one of the company's distributors to call and attempt to get an order.

The only problem was that there was no way of measuring Dan's performance or his contribution to the company. Dan knew this, and so did the general manager's assistant. When the general manager became ill and was away for an extended period, the assistant spoke to Dan about the situation.

Dan could see the handwriting on the wall and decided to find another job. In April 1966 he went to work for an electrocardiograph manufacturer as its salesman in the Midwest, with sole responsibility for the entire territory including Chicago. His salary was $12,000 a year and, for the first time, he had a company car. His assignment was to call on distributors of laboratory supplies.

Looking back, Dan thinks this was his favorite job. He had a boss that all salesmen dream about—one who says "Here's what we would like you to accomplish; how you do it is up to you." It's almost like being in business for yourself. In this position Dan learned the self-discipline that would later ease his transition from company man to manufacturers' representative.

In handling this job Dan also learned an important technique that is used by most reps: he learned to sell himself to his customers.

He had been taught in sales-training courses to sell the concept first, the product second, and himself last. This sophisticated approach often appeals to sales managers of large companies who frequently change their salesmen's territories. In such circumstance, the concept and product may be most important in selling. Since Dan was his company's only salesman in the Midwest, he decided to work on selling himself to his customers. He reasoned that if they knew and trusted him they would buy from him.

And that philosophy worked for Dan. Today many of those customers are his good friends and the mainstay of his rep business.

Dan's company employed a combination of direct-employee salesmen and manufacturers' representatives. Dan's first exposure to manufacturers' reps was when he had the opportunity of meeting Lee Walters, the company's southwestern representative and one of the leading medical reps in the country. Lee had also served as president of MANA (Manufacturers & Agents National Association). Prior to meeting Lee, Dan hadn't even known reps existed. Later Lee would counsel Dan about the complexities of the manufacturers' representative business, but at the time they met the furthest thing from Dan's mind was becoming a rep. He was a conservative person, happy to work on a straight salary for a good employer, and not at all anxious to work on a commission basis.

In the early 1970s it was obvious to Dan that his company was lagging behind in product development. He witnessed competitors easily taking orders that should have been his and felt it was only a matter of time before the company would be sold by its parent organization. In such an event, his job would definitely be in danger.

During that time he briefly thought about the rep business. But the reps he knew had impressed upon him the difficulty of obtaining good lines, and whatever interest he had was dispelled by their gloomy predictions.

Now living in Glen Ellyn, Dan and Norma had one child and Norma was again teaching. Dan decided to look for another job and soon found one, working as a Chicago-area salesman for an eastern company that manufactured highly sophisticated equipment for clinical labs in hospitals. Again, the product was sold to distributors, but it was so complicated that the company sales-men—rather than the distributor salesmen—did most of the demonstrating and selling.

Working for his new company led Dan to his first experience with quotas, and it was a real eye-opener. His quota for the first six months was quite low, and he easily surpassed it. The second six month's quota was raised, and he barely made it. When the third six months produced a much higher quota and a smaller territory, Dan understood the Catch 22 of quotas: If you make it, your quota is raised or your territory is cut. Dan's firm went one step further and did both.

Another obstacle was the fact that the top salesman and the No. 3 salesman in the company had previously worked his territory and had sold just about every product in his line to their customers. This left Dan with very little to sell. His company's products were ex-pensive machines for blood analysis and related functions, and once a hospital purchased one it seldom required another for years. Dan, making $16,000 a year with a bonus tied to his quota, was becoming extremely disillusioned with the constant pressure to produce.

At about this time, Dan was approached by a former boss who was distributing electrocardiograph paper. He asked if Dan would be interested in selling this paper to users in the Midwest. Though interested, Dan realized he couldn't do the selling on company time, and so he declined. Their second child had recently arrived and Norma, since she wasn't working at the time, suggested that per-haps she could handle the line by mail and phone. She didn't plan to teach while the child was still quite young and was eager to give the offer a try.

Although he didn't know it at the time, this decision would result in Dan's entering the rep business at a later date. He set Norma up as a representative of the paper firm, and they formed a company named NorDan Associates. Dan had no official connection with the firm and Norma was president.

She set about mailing letters to many of Dan's acquaintances and to customers of his former employers who were logical prospective customers. In the letter, she mentioned Dan's name and went on to outline the merits of their electrocardiograph paper. From time to time, Dan also picked up the phone and talked to several of the customers he had known particularly well, telling them of Norma's new venture. Most of them agreed to give her company a chance.

Soon the young business was taking in $300 a month, a tidy sum for an operation that had little overhead and could be worked from home. Dan was becoming increasingly disenchanted with his pressure-cooker job and he started to think more about Lee Walters and some of the other reps he knew who were doing well in their own businesses.

In 1973 Dan sat down one day with a copy of the trade journal *Surgical Business* and reviewed the ads. After eliminating advertisers such as Johnson & Johnson, which would obviously have its own direct sales force, he made a list of the companies he thought might sell through reps. He then had letters printed up on NorDan stationery soliciting these lines for representation, and mailed them a few days later. Actually, this was more or less a lark for Dan. While his interest in becoming a rep was growing, he simply didn't expect to receive any yes answers, mainly because the reps he knew had told him lines were difficult to obtain.

To his amazement two companies wrote back and said he could represent them in the Midwest. Dan decided this stroke of luck was too good to pass up, and he made plans to enter the rep business. Essentially, through Norma, he had been in the rep business part time with the NorDan operation, selling electrocardiograph paper. So he had the ideal vehicle for entering the business on a full-time basis.

When Dan started his own sales agency part time in August 1973, he had one essential ingredient that most new reps do not have—he had a *maintenance income.* Norma had gone back to teaching, and her salary, along with the $300 a month earned by NorDan plus about $200 a month in existing commissions from Dan's two new lines, gave the Jurgens family a monthly income of approximately $1,500—an amount they could live on and run a modest business.

If absolutely necessary, Dan could work evenings as a pharmacist in a local drugstore at $8.00 an hour. Over the years he had occasionally done this to have a few dollars to spend on his favorite sport, hunting.

This, then, is a maintenance income, and it was in keeping with Dan's security consciousness. He could begin his rep business without unduly concerning himself about reaching breakeven day.

When Dan gave his boss notice, there was dead silence. His company's Chicago office employed three salesmen, but one had just been transferred and the second had recently resigned. This left only Dan, and now he too was resigning. His boss asked him to think it over and come back the following morning.

The next day Dan's boss asked him to continue on at full salary for two months with the provision that he would accept specific assignments from the boss to demonstrate the company's equipment. There would be no quota to worry about, and Dan could use his company car on company business and pay for the gas when he needed it for his rep business. He could also continue to charge the company for any expenses he incurred because of company assignments. This was a stopgap procedure until new men could be hired by the company, but it worked well for Dan. During those two months he received only three half-day assignments and spent the rest of the time on his rep business.

Dan remembers well the last day he was officially employed. It was October 15, 1973, which also coincided with the opening day of deer season in Wyoming, and Dan was in Wyoming hunting deer. When he returned home October 25, he went full time into the rep business.

At that time Dan had three lines. He worked hard to develop business for his principals, and gradually his commissions began to build. He worked, and still does, through distributors, seldom making a call on the ultimate purchaser of his products. Many of these are the same distributors he worked with during his tenure as a direct salesman.

In 1974 Dan incorporated his business. He formed a regular corporation, a decision he now regrets. Later an adviser suggested a change to a Subchapter S corporation, which allowed Dan to be taxed practically as a sole proprietorship—using personal, instead of business, tax rates and applying any losses against personal income. However, he still has most of the advantages, as well as the disadvantages, of a regular corporation.

From the start Dan has always made enough money to cover his business expenses, but he hasn't really spent much time in the profit column. This is because he is developing his business in the manner that suits him best. He has no desire to have his sales agency grow into a large organization. He intends to remain a one-man business, and this is with the full knowledge of his principals.

For this reason he limits the number of lines he will carry and gives them his undivided attention. He is now building these lines and gaining a reputation as one of the Midwest's leading medical- and orthopedic-supply representatives. Because of this and one or two prospective lines with great potential, Dan expects to do very well financially in a year or two.

Although up to this point Dan hasn't turned an appreciable profit, he does make the most of the benefits that are possible through the judicious use of his corporate structure. Insurance, hospitalization, and other fringes are deductible expenses.

He also owns a motor home and during the summer travels throughout his territory—which now comprises Illinois, Wisconsin, Indiana, Ohio, and Michigan. He takes his family along and legally deducts expenses for his portion of the weekday travel. On weekends, when the Jurgens are usually parked at a resort area, expenses are personal and can't be deducted. Nevertheless, traveling in this manner is actually less expensive than renting a motel room every night, and it gives the family a chance to be together and enjoy the pleasures of vacation spots several hundred miles from home, too far away for an average weekend.

Dan also uses the motor home to display some of his products. Thus he accomplishes two objectives—he shows off his wares, some of which are too big to lug into an office, and he gets the undivided attention of the buyer. No phones ring, and there are no interruptions from the buyers' associates. Dan figures a half hour with a customer in his motor home is worth an hour and a half in the customer's office. Of course, with the price of gas going up and with supply becoming more uncertain, Dan has had to be much more careful in planning the use of his vehicle.

His present lines consist almost entirely of expendable products—products that are used up and have to be replaced at frequent intervals (such as the electrocardiograph paper)—as opposed to capital equipment (such as an electrocardiograph machine), which is purchased for long-term use. Commissions are usually less on expendables than on capital equipment, but selling is easier. Once a customer becomes used to purchasing from you, if you continue to offer competitive prices and prompt delivery, chances are he'll continue to buy from you on a regular basis.

Dan has also come up with an excellent promotion piece. Instead of handing out individual bits of literature, depending on whose behalf he is making a call, he has put together a very professional-looking loose-leaf binder illustrating all the product lines he carries. Each line has its own section, and every customer Dan calls on receives one of his binders.

He is one of the few reps I know, other than large agencies with many salesmen, who has gone to the trouble of presenting a very fine image of his agency, NorDan, Inc., and himself. Dan keeps a mailing list for special events or announcements and uses the list to his advantage—another good promotional idea.

Dan says that one of his biggest errors in the early years was his lack of insistence on a contract. He had handshake agreements with several of his principals and found out the hard way that if it's not down in writing it can cost you money. In several cases new sales managers were appointed, and the executives who had shaken his hand and made the verbal agreement were no longer with the company. Their successors usually had no knowledge of the original arrangements. Dan lost territories, had commissions cut, and suffered all kinds of inconveniences because he neglected to insist on a contract. He says he's learning, and he advises all new entries into the field to make certain they have a signed contract before they go out to sell a principal's products. With approximately six representatives in the greater Chicago area selling medical supplies similar to

Dan's, he isn't burdened with fierce competition and is looking forward to nice growth in a business he thoroughly enjoys.

ANALYSIS

Dan Jurgens is a mixture of many things; he's conservative, security conscious, independent, and insistent on a lifestyle that doesn't necessarily fit the image of the average rep. A good many reps look forward to the day when they can expand their agencies, add employees, and become managers instead of salesmen.

Dan isn't interested in building a large organization. He works hard for the few principals he represents, and he does as good a job for them as do larger sales agencies with many more lines to sell. When he takes on a new principal, he makes a point of describing his business philosophy. If he meets resistance, no arrangement is made. This makes Dan a better salesman since he doesn't have to pretend that he expects his firm to get bigger and better. He can go about his sales visits with a clear conscience.

Because of his concern for security—a common characteristic among reps—Dan started his agency under the best of all possible conditions; he made certain he had a maintenance income to carry him as long as he needed. Paul Rice also had extra income enabling him to work without undue concern about when breakeven day would arrive, but he worked nights and weekends to get it. Dan's additional income, provided by his wife and their part-time business, didn't involve any of his time outside regular working hours. Thus it was a true maintenance income. There was no pressure to make large initial sales in order to bring in enough money to maintain his business and his home. Actually, Dan was out hunting deer in Wyoming on the first official day of his new agency. How unconcerned can you get?

He also benefited from having his firm in business and operating a full year before he left his job. True, his wife was running it in her spare time, but it was an established business. Dan merely stepped into it and started making personal calls. This eliminated a lot of the start-up details and confusion that a new rep experiences at a time when he needs to devote his energies to finding good lines and selling them.

Dan's cautiousness is a good example for anyone who is unduly concerned about beginning his own sales agency. By having a maintenance income, no grandiose ideas of rapid expansion, and a firm that was already under way, he reduced his chances of failure to practically zero.

7
ART BYRNE
A Buyer
Goes Selling

In 1955 when I was a rather naive assistant sales manager for a steel-forging company in Chicago, it was all I could do to keep our reps supplied with prompt quotations from their customers. We had a fine group of sales agencies, most of which had been with the firm before I joined it in 1942 and were still with it when I struck out on my own in 1968, a real testimonial to both the reps and the company. But keeping up with them was almost more than one human could cope with, and I wound up doing most of my detail work after 5:00 p.m. Too often it was 7:30 or 8:00 before my wife could greet me with a martini and news of the day.

In the midst of a particularly hectic day, the president of the company came into my office and announced that he had appointed a new representative firm to handle our business in New York and New England. I threw up my hands in despair. Having too much to handle already, the thought of wet-nursing a new rep firm was more than a little discouraging. I was also certain we couldn't be competitive that far away from Chicago and could visualize the young agency flooding me with inquiries that would never turn into orders.

I told the president how I felt—diplomatically, of course—and though he noted my objections, he pointed out we had nothing to lose and that it would be worth a try.

It wasn't long before I heard from one of the partners of our new agency, Art Byrne. He phoned to introduce himself and to say he was sending in an inquiry and asked if we would quote as promptly as possible. When I hung up, I felt some sympathy for Art. He sounded like a hard worker, and I knew he would soon become discouraged by our noncompetitive quotes. Eight years later Art Byrne of Arthur G. Byrne Co., Inc., was bringing our firm one million dollars' worth of business a year. My business judgment, demonstrated by my assessment of Art's chances to succeed, was one of the reasons I was assistant sales manager and the president was the president.

Our president was undoubtedly the finest salesman I have ever been associated with, though he never spent a day in the sales department as far as I know. Once he was introduced to a customer, we in sales could breathe easy. He had a natural ability to make a customer want to do business with him. Obviously his talents also included recognizing a good rep when he saw one.

Art Byrne's story appears here because he is my idea of the complete professional rep. The other five representatives whose stories I've told have fewer years in the field and appear to be well on their way to successful careers, but Art has arrived. He is the perfect example for you, and for all of those who started within the last few years, to emulate. Another reason for telling Art's story is because he entered the field with no prior selling experience. His business career began on the buyer's side of the desk, and we'll see how valuable that experience can be. After reading about Art Byrne, those of you who are not now in sales-related positions but who want to be manufacturers' representatives will be encouraged to cast your lot with our profession.

During his years at Great Neck High School on Long Island, Art had a penchant for taking apart car and motorcycle engines and putting them back together. The fact that they seemed to run not only well but better than before, when everything was back in place, undoubtedly sparked his interest in things mechanical. Art's obvious flair for mechanical technology prompted him to his first entrepreneurial endeavor, the purchase and sale of autos and motorcycles. This, plus his studies, kept him busy until he entered Lehigh University. It would be natural to conclude that as a result of his high school success with automobile engines, Art would go into engineering or perhaps business administration.

But however much Art may have wanted to follow his engineering instincts, higher math proved to be a stretch beyond his capabilities. Without this aptitude the pursuit of engineering studies would have been fruitless. My own feeling is that even had he left Lehigh an engineer, he wouldn't have pursued that vocation long. Art is an innovative doer, and success in the field of engineering usually involves several years of apprenticeship in an engineering department, working out the details of an isolated portion of some product or process. This wouldn't have satisfied the natural technical curiosity of someone who had mastered the art of rebuilding engines at the age of 15 or 16.

Since Art has four brothers who took up the legal profession, he worked toward a degree in history and government, which was more in keeping with the family trend.

Bethlehem, Pennsylvania, the home of Lehigh University, is also the location of Bethlehem Steel Company's largest plant, and to help put himself through school Art worked there during several summers. The first two summers he was put in the open-hearth department where the steelmaking process begins. It is rugged work; tons of iron ore, scrap, and alloying products are melted in giant furnaces to produce steel, which is then poured into ingots for further processing into bars, billets, and sheet forms for sale to other manufacturers. Those manufacturers, in turn, further refine the material to make it into finished and semifinished products.

During his last two years in college Art worked the graveyard shift in the heat-treating department, again far from a white-collar job. Large billets are placed in furnaces heated to temperatures that turn the steel a cherry red. This heat, plus special cooling procedures, imparts specified physical characteristics to the steel in terms of hardness, ductility, and machinability.

With World War II in progress, Art emerged from Lehigh with his degree in March 1943 and promptly entered the Navy. After midshipmen's school he served as a deck-division officer aboard a minesweeper. For Art, fresh out of college with a degree in history and government and with the intention of studying law, to be given an appointment to an entirely unrelated role was typical of our Armed Services' talent for placing the man in the job best suited to the man and the service. But the Navy erred in Art's case; how were they to know that beneath that liberal arts background there lurked a mine of rich mechanical capabilities? Art, to the Navy's good fortune, as well as his own, was in exactly the right job. He was in charge of the operation and maintenance of the ship and its mechanical components, which would further educate him in the workings of complex machinery.

Late in 1945, after the peace treaties were signed, he was transferred to Detroit. The Navy had by then recognized that his mechanical ability would be helpful in plant clearance and contract terminations for war goods no longer required. With his new wife, he lived in Detroit for six months disposing of tools and machinery the Navy owned. After his discharge this experience made him eligible for a job with the War Assets Board, which was also selling off government-owned equipment and closing plants.

Art's job with the War Assets Board enabled him to resume his education, and he attended law school at St. John's University in Brooklyn at night for a year and a half studying toward his law degree. This proved too time-consuming, however, and he did not finish.

In 1947 most of the equipment-disposal work had been completed, and Art looked for a position in the private sector. His technical background and experience in the steel mills contributed to his finding a job as buyer with American Car and Foundry Company in New York City. The company, now a conglomerate known as A.C.F. Industries, at that time manufactured only railway passenger and freight cars. The first year Art purchased steel products for the six car-building plants owned by this large company. Then he was assigned to buying lumber for these plants and spent the next three years learning about the lumber business. The railway car-building business was and is particularly cyclical, and when the railroads weren't buying there were no alternative outlets for car-builders' products. Their suppliers, usually specializing in sales to car builders, were also subject to these big ups and downs; for this reason most of them sold through manufacturers' representatives. Art soon met his first rep, and through the years did millions of dollars of business with this group of independent salesmen. He saw the income possibilities open to an aggressive rep, but he didn't act on his observation.

Art had more important things on his mind. His experiences as a buyer made him an expert in procurement—not only in finding good-quality suppliers but also in negotiating the best deal. So at the start of the Korean War, Art and two associates at American Car formed an Army battle-tank-parts brokerage firm. With his knowledge of mechanical components and his previous experience with government specifications, Art found it easy to buy tank parts and resell them to the brokerage firm's customers. Some of the suppliers he approached insisted on selling the parts direct to the customer; in those cases a commission for Art's firm was included in the selling price quoted to the customer, since Art and his associates had made the original contact and did the actual selling. But wherever possible, Art's firm preferred to broker the parts rather than merely receive a commission; the profit was better. The contacts he made during the war, both with customers and suppliers, were to serve him well as the years passed.

One of Art's associates at the brokerage firm had provided most of the original capital and owned 60 percent of the company; Art and the second partner each had 20 percent of the business. When he left American Car in 1951, Art was making $5,000 a year; his salary at the brokerage firm was $5,500, certainly a respectable income for 1951. This figure went from respectable to grandiose when, in their second year of business, Art's share of the profits came to $25,000. This tremendous increase was partly due to the fact that the Korean War had heated up, and Art and his partners were able to sell a lot of ordnance parts.

When the war ended in 1953, the government's buying activities came to a screeching halt; so did the brokerage business. Plenty of material was available to buy, but demand had disappeared. With absolutely no market for the firm's talents, the brokerage business was dissolved and the majority owner went his own way.

Art and the second partner, however, had gotten a taste for being in business for themselves, and had already dabbled in the rep business as a part of the brokerage firm's activities. Since they had to eat, they decided to form a manufacturers' representative agency with offices in New York City.

Unfortunately, they didn't eat very well in 1954. Most of their potential customers were tooling up to convert their businesses and products back to a peacetime economy. If Art's firm had been selling tooling, he and his partner would have done quite well. But until customers were ready to make parts, which also required re-developing the market for their products, Art's new rep agency sold few goods. He tells of instances when buyers he called on simply said they weren't buying, before they even knew what Art was selling.

In 1955 industrial activity started to stir again. By this time the agency had added several lines that were to make the year an improvement over 1954. In particular, they landed a good customer for a new brass-casting line, a deal that was quite profitable. A once-in-a-lifetime break occurred when one of their principals was awarded a $10 million order for work on a 200-mile pipeline. At 5 percent commission this would have brought the two partners about $500,000. The principal, however, had made a serious error in estimating costs; the consequent loss experienced by the company was shared by the agency, and the final commission paid was only $5,000.

Art and his partner had every right to the full commission regardless of the company's error. But they realized that by enforcing the terms of the contract by law, they would most likely have dealt the company a serious financial blow—perhaps one that would have put it out of business. So they settled for the $5,000, a real disappointment. Even this amount helped, however, and by the end of 1955 each partner was able to realize about $5,000 after expenses—still not a bad income for those times.

Just as business was looking up, the agency experienced a major setback. The IRS instigated a major audit, skeptical that the agency's expenses could be so high in relation to the amount the partners drew. This is a common problem even today, because the average IRS agent usually understands sales expense only in relation to a manufacturing business where it amounts to 3 to 5 percent of total revenue; they become suspicious when they see this figure at 30 to 40 percent of total income. Of course, the higher ratio isn't unusual for a sales agency, because it has no manufacturing costs and little payroll expense. Almost all an agency's costs are related to travel and entertainment. Adding to the examining agent's suspicions was the fact that neither Art nor his partner had been particularly attentive to keeping good expense records. I am witness to the fact that the audit convinced Art that expense verification was mandatory, because I actually saw him collect receipts for even a 25-cent toll.

The result of the audit was a penalty for the partners that put such a dent in their rising expectations that Art knew he had to work much harder to make the agency successful. He didn't feel he could insist on an increased effort by his partner, who was ten years his senior; so late in 1956 they discussed the situation and agreed to phase out their partnership. Their arrangement had been to split the agency's profit 50–50 regardless of who brought in the business. To make the parting simpler and more expedient, they agreed to continue this arrangement through the following year—1957—and each would then officially open his own agency January 1, 1958.

This agreement gave both men the opportunity to work out the termination proceedings on a step-by-step basis and to cooperate with their principals in easing the transition, which is exactly what happened. In 1958 each went his own way, each retaining essentially the same principals for his own territory. The territories, of course, were not in conflict.

This was a real turning point for Art. He increased his pace considerably, taking advantage of all the experience he had gained over the past seven years. Up to this point he hadn't really been on his own, which may have affected his efforts to some degree, since whatever income he had been able to bring his firms had to be shared with others. Now completely independent, he was motivated to work not only harder, but smarter. At one time, his philosophy had held that the size of his results would be in direct proportion to the number of calls he made. There is, of course, a relationship; but Art discovered that, while the number of calls is important, the quality of the calls is the decisive factor for a successful salesman.

With his technical competence, Art would not merely visit eight factories a day and display his wares; he would also analyze each potential customer in advance and try to decide which of his lines would be the most logical to discuss with the purchasing personnel. If at all possible, he would acquaint himself with the prospective customer's product and approach the firm with a suggestion for improving, from an economical or design standpoint, one or more of the components that went into the company's product. This improvement, naturally, would be accomplished by the use of one of his principals' products.

Art also used good judgment when seeking principals. When he felt he needed a certain product to fill a void in his lines, he would survey the field of companies making that product. Then he would choose one or two of the leading candidates and phone or write the sales manager, outlining in detail what he could do for the company in his marketplace. This technique resulted in his obtaining better-than-average lines to represent.

By that time Art had associated himself with my firm and had also taken on a top-notch company out of Milwaukee. One of his major customers had started to tool up with both firms and was beginning to receive the forgings and castings the two companies manufactured. All of this, plus the sale of his other principals' products, brought Art's commissions for 1958 up to approximately $40,000 before expenses—a hefty increase over the previous year.

As Art's business grew, he faced many of the problems all businesses face as they increase their volume. Just as companies must add personnel to take care of increased business, reps must hire additional sales people to call on and service more accounts. Principals expect growth, and a rep reaches the point where he alone cannot make all the necessary calls.

Adding personnel in a sales agency, however, entails a risk not normally associated with the average company—that of eventual competition from the agency's own employees. Most firms gather assets as they grow—machines, tools, inventory, and cash reserves. This makes it difficult, but by no means impossible, for an employee to leave and start up a competitive firm. An employee taking this route incurs a tremendous risk, because he must accumulate capital and assets in order to set up shop and compete. All of this can be lost if his company doesn't get off the ground quickly.

An employee of a sales agency also must accept risk when leaving the agency to start his own business. But it is risk of a much smaller magnitude, and if he has a maintenance income—as Dan Jurgens did, for instance—he feels no undue pressure to succeed within a given period of time. Thus, already acquainted with the customers in his area from his previous experience with the agency, he can solicit competing lines and enter business for himself. Worse still, he can even go after the lines his employer represents.

If the rep, in order to avoid this eventuality, hires a less ambitious salesman—one who's likely to stick with the agency—he may find himself saddled with an unaggressive salesman who lacks the characteristics required to become a successful agency salesman.

Art, having built his business on a good strong base, wasn't particularly worried about this aspect of growth. He had confidence in his own ability to compete successfully regardless of the possibilities just mentioned, but he did need help at the agency.

In 1961 his brother, Bruce, was attending law school. Bruce was intrigued by Art's success, so Art suggested that Bruce join him at the agency while still in school to see whether he liked the business.

Bruce gave it a good try, but he decided that law interested him more.

Art then approached a former associate at American Car and Foundry about coming to work for him. The man agreed, and Art assigned the salesman the Long Island-New York City portion of his overall territory. He received 50 percent of the substantial commissions already accruing from that territory and 50 percent on new business that he developed. The man was an excellent salesman, and Art was very pleased with his progress.

In 1964 Art moved to Connecticut, in effect creating a second office for the agency since the salesman remained on Long Island. Before long, the salesman realized that he could handle another line or two. When he solicited a line that Art wasn't carrying, he realized that his action constituted moonlighting on Art's time, and he told Art what he had done.

Seeing the handwriting on the wall and realizing that his salesman would eventually take on other lines, Art suggested that each go his separate way. So in 1966 he was again handling the entire business alone.

Still seeking help, Art entered into an arrangement with another independent rep agency to handle part of his territory on a split-commission basis. The other agency had no competing lines, and so the agreement worked out quite well—on paper. But Art missed having direct control over the selling activities; he had no idea how much time the agency put in on his behalf and was aware, of course, that it could sell its own lines at higher commissions.

In 1969 the other agency, commonly known as a subagent in such a relationship, started taking on lines competitive to those carried by Art. This quickly ended the relationship, and Art went to a direct-employee basis and hired a salesman on a salary and bonus arrangement. The new salesman did a good job; again, however, after about three years the two parted, and the salesman later went into the rep business for himself.

Art finally decided it was time to go professional, even if it meant giving up part of the ownership of his agency. He negotiated with a top-notch executive of one of his customers. The man was vice-president of engineering for the firm and was well respected throughout his industry for both technical expertise and overall ability. He agreed to join Art's agency as executive vice-president with the opportunity to gradually assume part ownership of Arthur G. Byrne Co., Inc. The year was 1972.

Art's new vice-president was given a portion of the territory, but within months several good customers simply stopped buying for economic reasons. To make matters worse, for reasons beyond his control, the major customer in the executive's territory was lost almost overnight. Art had been counting on the commissions from this customer to pay most of the new man's substantial salary. This, plus the general business slowdown, reduced the agency's income drastically, and the vice-president decided to accept a position elsewhere.

Although business picked up dramatically the very next year, Art became somewhat discouraged about bringing in new personnel for a while, but his oldest son, Greg, showed an interest in the business and joined his father in 1975. Art sent him off to spend a few days at each principal's plant, and Greg came back with a beginner's knowledge of several different processes. Greg learned quickly and was soon selling and servicing customers in an assigned territory.

At about the same time, Art reestablished acquaintance with a former Lehigh classmate, a man who had been president of his family's nonferrous metal foundry for over 30 years. The foundry had run into union problems and other complications, causing its eventual demise. Art's acquaintance had then gone to work for an aluminum foundry on a salary-and-commission basis, and he arranged to sell for Art as a subagent. After a year Art concluded there was much to be gained by bringing this man on board full time. Art made him an officer of the agency, a lucky move, because in 1977 Greg left for other pursuits, and Art continued with his new associate.

Another problem that can face the established agency is the loss of profitable lines. This is seldom the result of the rep's inadequacies—usually a veteran agency selects its lines carefully and has a good chance for continuing prosperity.

In 1968 Art was doing a million dollars' worth of business for the company I worked for, but my company was experiencing serious problems. That year the forging division, which Art represented, was spun off by the parent organization and the new owners drastically reduced operations. Art lost from $40,000 to $50,000 a year in commissions. His other lines were going well, however, and—though this loss was difficult to swallow—it was by no means fatal to Arthur G. Byrne Co., Inc.

A few years later, in 1977 and early 1978, Art had a similar experience when one of his major principals started having financial problems. Contract negotiations were under way with the firm's union; a strike was called, the company's management gave up the ghost and declared bankruptcy. At the time this principal was considerably in arrears on accrued commissions and owed Art thousands of dollars, which he was unable to collect.

Art was able to find a firm making the same types of parts and shifted a portion of his business to it. But this company started having delivery problems, and he soon lost all the transferred business. This was quite a financial blow, but Art anticipated these losses. By obtaining additional principals and working harder, he was able to round out 1978 in good financial shape.

Art's story seems to have more downs than ups, but in reality the good years have far exceeded the bad for two reasons: Art didn't just *sell* to his customers; he *helped them solve their problems* and usually saved them money in the process; and he balanced his principals well, making certain that the loss of one or even two lines would not put him out of business.

After over 25 years of running a successful agency, the thing most surprising is that Art was discouraged by almost everyone, from college on, when he announced he would like to have a sales career. At Bethlehem Steel during college days, he asked for a transfer to the sales department and was turned down. His four years at American Car and Foundry were spent in futile attempts to get into the company's sales department. Finally, an employment counselor he consulted told him, "Mr. Byrne, will you please get it out of your head that you can be a successful salesman? You're simply not qualified."

Maybe, in a sense, all these detractors were right. Art doesn't fit the popular image of a salesman (which, incidentally, is a totally erroneous notion). He's pleasant to be with and an excellent host; but he seldom spends evenings around the bar with customers, nor does he indulge in other equally nonproductive activities often attributed to the successful salesman by people who don't really understand the salesman's function. Art does understand. He theorized that most buyers will purchase from someone who makes their job easier, is dependable, and can solve their problems. Art has been doing this very thing for many years, and his success is proof that it pays off.

ANALYSIS

I've told Art's story because it shows how perseverence and good sense can produce a long and successful career in this business. It wasn't easy for Art to reach his current level of income; he had many problems and many reverses. But by planning ahead and seeking lines that fitted his capabilities exactly, he has made himself invaluable to his customers and his principals. In the rep business, this is vital. By following Art's philosophy, you can gradually become the agency that customers turn to when they have problems in your field. Art's buyers don't need to bring in three or four different suppliers to help them determine what type of casting or forging to buy. Chances are Art has seen a similar problem in the past and can easily recommend the proper process to use. And since he has a company to fit almost any process needed in the casting or forging industries, he usually winds up with an order.

When you reach the point of self-sufficiency in your agency, keep Art Byrne's story in mind. To maintain a successful agency and to continue growing, you must work hard; but true success will come only if you also work smart.

8
DO YOU HAVE WHAT IT TAKES?
A Checklist for Success

NOW THAT YOU'VE seen how six men became successful manufacturers' representatives, you have no doubt been able to identify with some of their early experiences. Perhaps you've been working as a buyer, much the same as Art Byrne; or maybe you've been a direct-employee salesman or sales manager like Paul Elkin, but you know that, out on your own as a manufacturers' rep, you can increase your income dramatically.

Career experiences such as these are bona fide incentives for you to think harder about striking out on your own. After all, successful as they are, none of these reps are supermen; they're ordinary people just like you and me. I know; several of them have been my business associates and friends for years, and I have spent hours interviewing others. During earlier careers, these men developed certain characteristics that improved their chances of success in the independent sales field.

If you possess some of these traits, you too will have an excellent opportunity to succeed. Too many would-be reps don't fully understand that certain informal criteria are practically essential to the successful career of a rep. Those who do appreciate this need may be somewhat confused about the personality makeup required to give them a better-than-average opportunity to make the grade.

There is no one personality profile that automatically qualifies as perfect rep material. The reps I know have many different personalities. Some are friendly, outgoing, and persuasive. I know a number who are not particularly engaging but who have other traits that are equally important. However, despite the disparate surface impressions given by reps at a seminar or in a customer's reception room, there are similarities that can't be perceived just by visual observation. Even talking to a rep at length won't necessarily reveal those characteristics that give him an advantage over other hopeful candidates for the agency-sales business.

Most of the important characteristics are in the areas of attitude and discipline rather than physical attributes. Only by knowing and associating with this independent breed can you hope to gain insight into these unique traits.

Since that would take months—perhaps years—even if you were fortunate enough to know several reps, there is another method by which you can decide if you have a personality profile similar to that of most reps who have started and succeeded in their own businesses.

I've selected what I consider to be the major characteristics of the person with a better-than-average chance for success. These characteristics aren't drawn from any test results conducted by professional psychologists; I don't believe that such tests could be conclusive because of the widely varying personalities of the people in our field. Instead these are traits that I've observed over the years while working with reps, first as a sales manager and in more recent years as a full-time manufacturers' rep.

I've attended numerous sales meetings where, at the end of a day's activities, reps have met for dinner and have let their hair down, discussing everything from factory relations to tax shelters. At these informal discussions where a man feels at ease with his peers, it's much easier to assess the real qualities of an individual.

Over dinner or at the bar, most businessmen enjoy comparing notes, and reps are no different. Their profession has its own idiosyncracies, and sales meetings provide ideal opportunities for the exchange of information and experiences.

One interesting trait common to every successful rep I've ever met is confidence. I've never known a rep who not only was positive that he was in the right business but also was certain that his views on how to run his agency, how to work with his principals, and how to sell his customers were absolutely correct. This super-confidence is ingrained in these men. That's why rep seminars are so much fun to attend. When a subject is tossed out by the seminar leaders, there is no shortage of reps eager to critique the topic from beginning to end. Views naturally differ, but the absolute conviction held by each rep that *his* way of handling the situation is the *only* way leads to very lively discussion. This is in contrast to a seminar for sales managers, where those taking part are seeking the best way to do a job; though some may be on an ego trip, most participants spend their time listening to the formal presentations rather than explaining the infallibility of their own policies and actions.

Do you need confidence to begin you own agency? Yes, a confident approach is necessary for almost any venture you would undertake. But don't be concerned if you're not gifted with super-confidence at this point; that comes later, with experience. Most of the men who attend the seminars I mentioned are veterans, and their convictions come with years of experience and success in the rep business. To their credit, they're at the seminars because, despite their super-confidence, they know that something can always be learned from one's peers.

I've mentioned this trait because it seems to be the one essential prerequisite for starting your own business. If you don't yet have confidence, perhaps spending another year or two in your present job, or in investigating the field more thoroughly, will bring you to the point where you are certain of your own ability to break out on your own.

There are, of course, a number of other traits that are important to the successful rep. Let's discuss these in detail.

Are You Optimistic?

It's easy to confuse confidence with optimism. The former, however, is a result of experience and the latter is more truly a state of mind—a good state of mind and a great aid to the prospective rep.

Anyone in sales has to be optimistic, and one who is venturing into an untried area should have an extra measure. Those of you now working at sales jobs are aware of the need to look at the bright side of things. When Paul Elkin began thinking about getting into the rep business, he had confidence in his ability to sell his prospective principals' goods; but with no principals to represent, Paul had to be optimistic about his chances to attract those principals. Without this optimism he probably would never have written that first letter to a prospective principal. Paul Rice needed even more optimism, since he left his sales-agency job before trying to sign up his first principal.

As you take on line after line, you'll need to be optimistic about your learning ability. While most lines you will carry will be compatible, there can be important differences between them. You'll have to feel you can absorb the product knowledge required for the successful sales results your principals will expect.

Those of you without experience in sales who think you can make it in this business will need an even healthier dose of optimism. If you're quick to become discouraged or give up on a project that shows little promise, you should review carefully whether or not you have the temperament to venture on untried waters. However, the mere fact that you're reading this book is proof that you are by nature somewhat optimistic. You believe you can succeed in a career that has some meaning for you, and you're willing to learn as much as possible about it. That's a good sign.

Are You Realistic?

Optimism has got to be based on reality. If you don't have the ability to see things as they are and not as you'd like them to be, you may be getting into the wrong business. If you imagine a career that consists of occasional sales calls, long lunch hours, dependable principals, competitive prices, and walk-in business, you should stop and take another look.

If the rep business were easy, everyone would be in it. In truth, it's a tough, demanding occupation. You'll have some good principals and some who are not so good. Their quality and competitiveness will vary from company to company. Keeping all these balls in the air at one time can be exhausting and sometimes discouraging.

You have to recognize that those who succeed do so because they are able to deal in everyday reality and know they have to work hard and conscientiously to keep customers and principals happy. Orders do not just fall in your lap; quotations have to be followed up or the orders will go to competitors. Deliveries must be expedited or customers will become dissatisfied, and a constant watch must be mounted on your principals' pricing to keep your agency competitive. Lack of reality can be a handicap in the initial phase of your operation.

Many people have tried the rep field without truly assessing their chances for success. Two casual acquaintances formed a partnership and quickly signed up a number of lines. They also hired a secretary and signed leases for two big cars and a fancy office. Since the early days of a rep business are notoriously lean—it takes time to become established, sell the goods, and finally receive commissions—this pair barely got off the ground before they were shot down. Big front-end expenses and too little front-end income soon killed their business.

I cite an instance like this not to alarm you but to prepare you. It was apparent to most observers that this duo would have a hard time. If you have a realistic outlook, it will be obvious to you that this is not the way to start a new business.

There are hundreds of questions to ask yourself, but if you are realistic most of them won't be necessary. Realistic people have a "feel" for what they can and cannot do. This trait is vital to your success, not only in that first year, but in the years to come when your organization grows and important decisions must be made correctly if you are to prosper.

Can You Persevere?

As a salesman an occasional order will fall into your lap or come in over the transom, but the bulk of your business will come from your own pursuit of a potential order until you have it in hand. Every salesman must have this type of perseverance; without it, another vocation would seem to beckon.

In addition to perseverance in the selling function, you're going to need perseverance to hold out through that first year or two against tough odds. Some of you will find a couple of lines that will bring in a few quick dollars or that will have existing business in the area and commissions to match. Others, the majority, will find the going slower and will face a longer wait before attaining any kind of reasonable income base from which to operate.

In both cases perseverance is the order of the day. The luckier rep will have some income almost immediately, and—although it may not be sufficient for him to continue operating indefinitely—he may begin to feel that other income-producing breaks are just around the corner. Usually they aren't, without hard work. The old saying "The harder I work, the luckier I get" was never truer. The rep must continue chasing new lines and persevere until he has a diverse and solid group of compatible companies to represent.

The rep who starts with no lines, or only a few, clearly needs even more perseverance; if he's to succeed, he can't relax and hope that the needed lines will just appear. He must persevere in all areas to make this happen and it can take years. Our agency took five years to find and land the eight fine companies we now represent. Whether it takes more or less time depends partly on luck, but mainly on perseverance.

A good example of this involves a rep who had been in business for about a year when an excellent opportunity presented itself. He responded to an ad placed by a company looking for a rep in his area. He was interviewed by a sales manager who was himself new to the company and who was apparently quite favorably impressed by the rep's qualifications. The sales manager told him that the choice was between him and a larger rep agency, but he pointed out that his own position with his firm was somewhat dependent upon his lining up good professional reps, and were either of the two final candidates to fail to produce, he would receive much less management criticism if he appointed the old, established firm. This kind of frank and honest admission was admirable, but it was understandably disheartening to the rep. As it happened, the sales manager played it safe and appointed the larger firm. There went $12,000 in yearly commissions on existing business, as well as an excellent opportunity for a much greater income through conscientious sales work.

But this rep persevered. He knew that a personal problem of one of the principal partners of the firm that got the appointment was resulting in rapidly deteriorating sales performance, so he kept in touch since he felt it would be only a matter of time before the company realized its error.

Over the next 18 months, the rep dropped the sales manager a note when he found an interesting item in a trade journal or to compliment him on a particularly effective advertisement. The two men had taken a liking to each other, and this correspondence did not appear out of line. Also, adhering to the ethics of professional reps, he avoided trying to woo the line away from the appointed agency. He merely wanted his name to be remembered when the day for the decision to change reps came.

That day arrived about a year and a half after the original appointment, and a breakfast meeting at the airport was all that was necessary to negotiate a contract. Today, a few years later, the rep is realizing yearly commissions from that firm alone of approximately $55,000. Perseverance paid off.

Perseverance doesn't necessarily mean hard work; it means a determination to continue trying in the face of odds that may seem insurmountable. It's sticking to a course until action in your favor is consummated or the project is irrevocably decided in another's favor. In the latter case, perseverance becomes a waste of time and should be redirected to situations where there is a realistic chance of success.

Do You Have Self-Discipline?

Self-discipline is common among direct-employee salesmen. Most of them are out early, make their required rounds, and bring in the necessary number of sales. But in many such cases, it is a characteristic controlled by the sales manager through his discipline of his salesmen. He uses typical control devices, as he must. There is always the threat of being fired if such basics as promptness and good appearance aren't maintained. Self-discipline is also promoted through long-standing sales incentives such as raises, promotions, contests, and quotas. Without these incentives, most direct-employee sales people wouldn't perform as well as they do. The reasons are varied and perhaps best left to the business psychologists. The few who perform well with only ordinary incentives are potential reps, because they have self-discipline—the key to success.

This trait is necessary in all phases of a rep's business. Getting out of the office and making calls is, of course, the most basic type of self-discipline. Without that, all else is academic. But that's only the tip of the iceberg. Once commissions start flowing in, self-discipline takes on new meaning. A bigger car, a larger office, a trip to Hawaii—all are easy to justify. But when a bad year comes along, the bank account looks like Grand Canyon. The lack of self-discipline in the administration of your business can take you swiftly down the road to bankruptcy.

On the other hand, with self-discipline and restraint, the pleasure of having a nice car, an attractive office, a trip to Hawaii, and other perks or fringes can be increased tenfold by the knowledge that their cost comes from retained earnings rather than from current commissions. Retirement, too, if it is to be successful and comfortable instead of a stressful experience, must be planned for from the beginning of your business. In a later chapter we'll explore the details of retirement possibilities available to the self-employed.

Self-discipline becomes a real problem if you run your business from your home. There's always a chore undone around the house, and since you are your own boss, there's no need to be at the office at 8:00 A.M. It's easy to putter around the house taking care of minor obligations. One rep I know has the most attractive lawn in his neighborhood because of his daily care. Too bad his P&L statement doesn't look as good.

If you have a penchant for self-discipline, you'll have a good chance of succeeding. If self-discipline comes hard for you, practice it daily in your present occupation until you are convinced you've mastered it.

Paul Elkin was fortunate. While employed by the eastern conglomerate, he worked from his home where almost everything about his job resembled the routine of a rep. He had no difficulty disciplining himself to do his job completely and effectively, five days a week. Most people don't have that opportunity, so they must make doubly sure they possess enough self-discipline to justify taking the plunge.

Are You Security Conscious?

Most good reps are quite security conscious. If you're working for a company—large or small, it matters not—you probably have a lot less financial security than the average established rep. Sure, you have hospitalization insurance, life insurance, profit sharing, and a pension fund. But most of these fringe benefits would disappear if you lost your job. Unfortunately, in these days of mergers, acquisitions, management consultants, and a fickle marketplace, the loss of employment may have nothing to do with your ability to do your job effectively and efficiently.

Many company and corporation employees are terminated these days because—after a merger, for instance—only one sales manager is required. Or a new computer might take over the functions of an entire department. Having the benefit of a new service called "outplacement," designed to help you psychologically adapt to the shock of being fired, doesn't really help too much; you're still out of a job.

On the other hand, the successful rep can't lose his job, because he's not working for any one company. True, if he becomes lazy or ineffective, he can lose his lines one by one until none are left, but this would happen over a period of time, and the loss of a line or two would send up early-warning flags encouraging him to revert to his previous diligence and its effective results.

My contention, after observing many reps and listening to their questions at several seminars, is that good reps have a built-in security consciousness. Usually it was one of the main driving forces behind their determination to start their own sales agencies.

Certainly risk was involved. But in their minds, the initial risk was overbalanced by the possibility that in a few years they would have control over their own destinies rather than have their futures decided by a company or corporation.

How Are Your Bookkeeping Skills?

The chief accountant for a New York corporation, on arriving at his office every morning, would go straight to his desk, unlock his middle drawer, and glance at a piece of paper for a second or two. Then he would close the drawer, lock it, and go about his work.

He was struck down by a heart attack one morning as he reached the office. His subordinates did all they could for him, but when it was apparent he was beyond hope, they removed his keys and rushed to his desk to satisfy their curiosity about his morning ritual. In the middle drawer, they saw only one piece of paper. On it was written "The debit side is the one near the window."

Hopefully, your knowledge about the debit and credit sides of a ledger is a bit stronger than that. Numerous casualties occur among new reps because of their ignorance of financial matters. Some of them actually believe that whatever amount is shown in the bank balance at the end of the month is profit.

You need not major in accounting to go into your own business, but without some rudimentary knowledge of finance and taxes you'll find the early stages very difficult. Check out the library for a few books on small business finance. Your requirements will be rather simple, and you should be able to absorb the fundamentals easily. In the next chapter you will be given suggestions on how to avoid expensive accounting fees in the first year or two through the use of prepared forms available at your local office-supply store. However, if this is an area that you simply don't understand, then money spent on a bookkeeping service will more than pay for itself.

Let's not kid ourselves; independence and freedom of action are great features of being in business for yourself, but money is the name of the game, and absolutely no risks should be taken with this valuable commodity. If you can't keep your own finances straight, find someone who can—perhaps your wife—and then follow the advice you receive.

Do You Have a Flair for Promotion?

You need the ability to promote yourself and your agency for the purpose of attracting lines as much as for selling products. Your solicitation for a line, particularly a good one, will be judged against some pretty heavy competition. Without good lines to represent, you will, of course, have nothing to sell. Some promotional ability is necessary if you are to make your efforts to obtain a line stand out in favorable contrast with the other reps competing for that line.

A well-composed neatly typed letter on a good letterhead, a few testimonials, a small brochure—all these create a good first impression. Don't settle for a poorly written letter typed on a machine needing a new ribbon.

Advertisements for lines in trade journals and other business publications must have some flair if they are to be noticed. Even if you employ a free-lance agency, you still must be able to direct the message so that it presents its *sell appeal* to the right party.

After obtaining those good lines, you will also need promotional talent to sell against competing reps and direct-employee salesmen. Even today, too few reps engage in good advertising and promotional activities; those who do have a definite edge over their competitors.

And your sales appeal must also be evident at the personal level. When a prospective principal's sales manager comes to town to interview, he's going to be interested in whether or not you can sell him on appointing your agency to represent his company.

Phone him on the day of the appointment to make sure he's arrived and the interview is still on. You'll be one of the few reps to do this. Arrive promptly and phone again from the lobby to make certain he's ready to see you. Little courtesies like these impress any good sales executive because it indicates dependability.

How you perform during the actual interview will be the deciding factor, and here you're on your own. As a successful salesman, you know what it takes to sell your company's products, and the same strategy should be followed during the interview because, after all, you're trying to sell yourself. If you're a good salesman you'll do well in the interview, and selling yourself in this situation can be one of the most profitable sales you'll ever make.

Are You Tactful?

Sometimes a rep's diplomacy is even more important with his principals than with his customers. You'll be representing and dealing with seven to ten different companies and their personnel. How well you get along in these varied relationships can often spell the difference between failure and success.

For instance, what good is an order from a favorite customer if your company can't ship it out promptly? Perhaps you irritated the production control manager by going over his head once too often, and he got even by scheduling your order on an overburdened machine where delivery of parts is hopelessly behind schedule.

A rep faces more of these problems than the direct salesman, because the rep is seldom at the plant, and internal politics can change drastically from one visit to another. An executive can quickly go out of favor without your knowing it, and internal dissension can be unintentionally caused if tact and responsiveness are not practiced with your principals at all times.

One veteran southeastern rep lost a $35,000-a-year line because of his continual carping about one of the company's policies. A capable salesman in every other way, his lack of tact in running a dead horse into the ground finally so irritated the company's executives they reluctantly terminated him.

Tact requires insight into the attitudes and feelings of others, and this will be doubly difficult for you because of your remoteness from the principals' facilities. Without being on the scene, you can't witness the subtle changes that take place in a company's internal politics and policies.

Professional reps often make a practice of visiting principals' plants at least once a year to keep their finger on the pulse of the companies' activities. This is a good practice to keep in mind after you've built your business to the point where the expense of such trips won't impose a financial strain on your resources.

Are You a Good Manager?

You must also be a good manager, even though you may be a one-man agency for years. A manager has the ability to make important decisions concerning the various facets of his operation. Here are a few questions that will come up.

When do you hire your first employee? You're busy and getting busier; paperwork is falling behind and obligations are piling up. Is it important to hire a part-time employee to take care of this backlog and then have less funds to run the business? Or is it better to struggle along and use those same funds to travel more and keep your customers and principals happy?

How do you select an attorney and accountant? These two professional advisers can often make or break your business, depending upon the quality of their advice. The attorney next door might be happy to advise you, for a fee, about whether to incorporate or stay a sole proprietor. He or she might also specialize in divorce cases and not really be capable of providing the best advice for your situation. Your neighbor on the other side may be an accountant for a large CPA firm, anxious to pick up a few extra dollars moonlighting for you. Unfortunately, the closest exposure this accountant may have had to small business accounting was when he did a case study as a second-year college student. In this instance, the accountant's advice can send you off on the wrong road—to financial difficulty. Choices in these two fields will tax your managerial capabilities.

Should you appoint subagents? This can be a tricky and sometimes tempting device to cover more area and accounts than you can do alone, but the decision to do so can have an important impact on your relations with your principals. Some arrangements of this type have worked out well, but it's possible that the need for a decision of this nature may come up before you'd like it to.

These and other questions will crop up with regularity. How you answer them will go a long way toward deciding the future health of your business.

Are You Entrepreneurial?

If you have given affirmative answers to most of the questions in this chapter, the chances are good that you have the makings of an entrepreneur—and only entrepreneurs will make a success in the rep business.

Entrepreneurs are not perfect and are not always right in their decisions, but the cardinal rule is to be right more often than wrong. It also helps a lot if you're right on the important things and wrong on the minor ones. Knowing which is which is a typical trait of an entrepreneur.

If you feel a little thin on some of the more important qualifications of the entrepreneur, do your homework. Go to the library and study the subjects that need polishing. Pay attention to articles on small business—more and more of them are appearing daily in various publications. Find out all you can about the rep business, which is what this book is all about.

9
FINAL PREPARATIONS
Countdown
to Independence

You HAVE NOW read the checklist for success. Since you are beginning this chapter, you apparently feel you have the qualifications to become a manufacturers' representative. Fine, but don't hand in your resignation yet. A number of essentials must be carefully planned for and thought through before you make that final, irrevocable commitment.

How Much Capital Investment?

This question is as critical as it is difficult. Trying to figure out how much capital you will need to reach breakeven day is hard because there are so many variables in this business.

For instance, off-the-shelf items, such as those sold by Dick Cole, can bring in commissions in 30 to 60 days. Total commissions for these items ordinarily grow much faster than will commissions for

Paul Elkin's products, which have to be individually engineered and consequently require a much longer delivery lead time, resulting in a longer wait for commissions. Witness the first- and second-year earnings of Dick versus Paul—Dick, $25,000 and $55,000; Paul, $10,000 and $28,000.

Here are several questions to ask to help you determine your need for capital:

- Do you already have a good following in your chosen territory?
- Do your prospective principals make products that can be readily sold, or will considerable missionary work have to be done?
- What are the standard commission rates for your proposed lines?
- What will be the estimated yearly operating expenses of your agency?
- What yearly income can your family realistically live on?

Only you can take these figures and attempt to forecast how much capital will be needed to take you to breakeven day. All I can offer is a word of caution—don't underestimate. Nothing is more discouraging than to "almost make it." If you run out of money just short of breakeven day, it will result, at worst, in a total loss of your investment or—at best—in a drastic dilution of ownership in your agency caused by selling a majority interest. The extra reserve, perhaps only a few thousand dollars, can mean the difference between a successful career as a manufacturers' rep and a trek back to company employment offices.

By noting the beginning capital investments of the reps mentioned in the earlier chapters who started in recent years, and by considering a yearly inflation rate of 5 to 8 percent, you can compare your estimated figures with theirs—noting, of course, similarities and differences between their product lines and those of your prospective principals.

Don't overlook the differences in territory, following, age, and experience.

Where Do You Find Investment Capital?

Seldom at the bank.

Some of my best friends are bankers, but their willingness to take a chance on a beginning rep is similar to their eagerness to honor a check on an overdrawn account. Collateral, of course, is the name of their game, but even with attractive collateral your neighborhood banker is probably not in a rush to lend funds to a newly established rep. Bankers honestly don't relish repossessing homes or cars and prefer to see a steady paycheck coming in before they open the checkbook.

However, if you're fortunate enough to have a good relationship with your banker, and if you also have plenty of collateral, you may be able to obtain a loan. If so, there are several things you can do to make payments easier if money gets tight temporarily.

You can request a term or commercial-pay loan. If your banker is willing, this means you can wait up to 90 days for repayment or even longer. Also, interest on this type of loan is computed daily, so if you strike it rich and want to pay it off, you'll be charged for the interest to date only. By contrast, the installment type of loan is figured on the principal and interest for the duration of the loan. This is then divided into the term of your loan (36 months, for instance) with 1/36th due each month. In the event you wish to pay it off early, you still must pay 36 months' interest, less a small prepayment refund.

It's not unusual for relatives and family members to aid new reps in the form of loans. Paul Mitchell received an $8,000 loan to help him continue his winning course. As in the case of Paul, frequently this type of loan is more readily available after the success of a venture is apparent.

Another way a credit-worthy relative can be of assistance is to co-sign or guarantee your loan at the bank. If his or her credit rating with the bank is excellent, this is often a good method of obtaining funds more easily or for receiving a larger loan than what the bank would give you without such a guarantee.

If you own a home and have paid off a good portion of your

mortgage, refinancing the mortgage represents perhaps the best source of substantial funds. Paul Elkin, for instance, raised $17,000 in this manner and Dick Cole a similar amount. In some states, however, banks are prohibited from refinancing homes to provide business capital because of a homestead act. Of course, you can sell your home and buy a smaller one or rent an apartment.

Savings may be put to use, and there are also funds that you may be eligible to receive from your current employer when you resign your position. Many companies have profit-sharing plans and employee-contributory pensions. A portion of these funds is available to the employee upon retirement, termination, or resignation.

A part-time job, while somewhat incongruous for a new agency owner, is a convenient way to stretch your income sources to a point six months to two years beyond your projected breakeven day.

If you're really serious about achieving independence and a career that will eventually produce an attractive income, you'll have to accept the fact that the early days of your newfound independence may require a sacrifice that will appear to be beneath your accustomed responsibilities and income. If your talents are equal to your confidence, these sacrifices will be short-lived, and you will soon be able to leave your part-time chores and spend full time at being a successful manufacturers' representative, as Paul Rice did.

The best of all worlds, of course, is the maintenance-income plan. Through this route, your success is virtually assured. But it's not easy and it requires sacrifices from you and your entire family. A maintenance income, remember, is different from income from a part-time job that uses your personal energies. It is a separate independent income. It can be a combination of contributions—income through an inheritance, a full-time job by your wife, and paper routes by the kids. You then add up the dollar amounts of these contributions and scale down your living expenses accordingly.

Adapting your standards to a more modest income than you are accustomed to is vital to the maintenance-income plan; if the family as a group or any individual member is not ready for this style of living, then the plan will fail. It's tough, but it can be accomplished with a minimum of fuss if the ultimate rewards are worth it to your family—a better college for the kids and a more flexible, affluent lifestyle for the entire family.

The best way to handle this situation is to put your intentions up front. Tell friends and relatives that you're going into your own business and that your lifestyle will be undergoing a temporary change. You will of course be happy to have them over for hamburgers on a Sunday afternoon, but the occasional dinners at swank, expensive restaurants will have to wait for another day.

The reward for you comes immediately. You can forget financial worries and concentrate 100 percent on getting your business started. You can be relaxed when visiting a potential customer instead of trying too hard for an order.

Look at Dan Jurgens. Even when I visited him, three years after he started as a rep, he wasn't too concerned with making it; he had it made the day he started in his own business with a maintenance income of $1,500 a month. Dan, although admittedly conservative, was relaxed, and with this attitude he is building a very successful business.

Aside from strong entrepreneurial instincts, the one biggest need for a beginning rep is sufficient capital, through one method or another. No one should attempt to become a manufacturers' representative without assurance that the funds are available.

What's in a Name?

If you open your local Yellow Pages to the listing for manufacturers' representatives, you'll probably get the distinct impression that reps are an egocentric breed. Why? Because almost every one of them uses his own name when choosing a name for his sales agency.

Well, perhaps some of them are ego-oriented, but the real reason for this apparent self-centeredness has its roots in a very useful business practice—identification. If a business is to succeed, its customers *must* remember its name. This is the reason for the expensive advertising campaigns of major corporations such as IBM, Kodak, and 3M. The constant repetition of these identifying symbols over television and in all other media is designed to imprint the name of the firm in the buyer's subconscious so that when a need for a product arises, the buyer is conditioned to purchase the product of the company whose name is familiar.

There are light-years of difference between your opportunity to advertise and that of such companies as IBM, Kodak, and 3M, but the philosophy behind the promotional programs of these companies is not far removed from your own business philosophy—at least it shouldn't be. When starting your own business your name may be the best asset you have. It's a form of identification that no one else possesses, and you must make it work for you.

Odds are good that you're setting up your business in a territory where you have numerous business acquaintances. If you're now a salesman, these people will be customers that you've worked with in the past. If you're a former buyer or engineer, you'll know many people through professional business associations sponsored by each individual society. If you've built up recognition in the area through these groups, why throw it away? By using your own name in your business you'll build on that recognition, and that's an important plus in getting through the starting gate at a gallop.

Even if you haven't established visibility in the area, it pays to seriously consider using your own name in the title of your business. Your customers need remember only one name, not two. If your name is Henry Atkinson and you call your agency Leisure-Time Products, you are asking your customers to remember both names. Naturally, you want them to remember your name first. But when they get around to placing an order, it's an even bet they'll have trouble recalling the first few times exactly where to send it. Make it simple for them. It'll be a lot easier for a buyer to remember Henry Atkinson Associates than for him to recall both names. All of your promotional energies can then be directed toward establishing the name of Henry Atkinson Associates. In these early days, instant recognition will be essential to the fast start-up of your business.

In the case of a partnership, you may wish to consider using what is called an assumed name—a company name that does not make use of your own name in its title. If you're entering business with an associate, it's assumed that the partnership will last a long time. But things don't usually work out that way; most partnerships are changed from time to time, either because of disagreements or by the addition of other partners. Within the space of a few years Henry Atkinson Associates can change to Pierce & Atkinson Associates, Pierce Atkinson & Johnson Associates, and then perhaps back to Henry Atkinson Associates. All of these changes can cause the very confusion you tried to avoid by sticking to your own name. The lack of consistent identification can also be a serious drawback to increasing sales.

When my partner and I formed our agency, we decided on an assumed name. Initially, we had thought of calling our company Momentum, Inc., but when we found out that incorporation would entail our shelling out $400 in lawyers' fees, we changed the name to Momentum Sales.

It didn't take long to learn that this wasn't going to work. When we presented our business card to a receptionist, she would take it to the buyer and immediately come back out and ask what we were selling. After repeated time-wasting excursions, we decided to remedy this problem by renaming our agency Momentum Metals, which at least gave the customer a hint of what was in store for him.

By failing to realize the importance of coming up with a practical name when we started our sales agency, we were forced to change all our business records, cards, stationery, and bank accounts—a real nuisance and, worse yet, an expense that we could ill afford in the early days of our agency.

So think carefully about the name you choose for your business. Hopefully, you'll be stuck with it for a long time.

About Partnerships

Historically, partnerships don't work out. There is a simple reason for this. Two friends decide it would be just great to carry their successful personal relationship one step further, into a business relationship. This is probably one of the leading causes for the breakup of friendships.

A number of years ago three of my close friends and I started a part-time business selling a patented device produced by a rather parsimonious manufacturer. As time went on we became fairly successful. We found, however, that while we could easily agree on matters such as what golf course to play or where to go for dinner, it was surprisingly difficult to make collective decisions on business matters. So we had meetings, and soon we were spending more time in meetings than we were in selling the product. An important reason for our inability to make simple decisions was our dissimilar business backgrounds. Each of us looked at the problems from his own point of view and business experience, and the viewpoints were not at all alike.

Fortunately, this was a part-time business, and the income was not necessary for our financial well-being. Finally, the manufacturer sold his patent to another company and we were terminated, which was probably the best thing that could have happened for the sake of our friendships.

Partnerships consisting of two or more friends may create more heat than light, but some partnerships that are formed on a different basis offer excellent chances for success. These are relationships established where the partners have the same business background, especially when both partners have worked for the same company or organization. Each company has its own basic philosophy and way of doing business, and this rubs off on its employees; they naturally tend to view business actions from the same general point of view. My partner and I, having been together for ten years with no major conflicts, are inclined to attribute our ability to function well together to the fact that we both worked for the same company. We generally agree on most of the problems that face us and we approach the selling, promotional, administrative, and financial sides of our business the same way.

On the whole, my recommendation is to go it alone. You're entering this business partially for the independence it offers, and with a partner all major decisions must be shared. A sales agency is particularly vulnerable because funds may be restricted, and the policy regarding the allocation or distribution of those funds can be a constant source of dispute. In a recent survey of professional sales agencies, only 4 percent were listed as partnerships, which should tell you something.

What Form Should Your Business Take?

Many new rep organizations set up immediately as corporations on the advice of an attorney. Art Byrne did, but his brothers were lawyers; your brother may be a building contractor. If you have the money and can afford the several hundred dollars in legal fees it takes to become incorporated, you may want to consider that. Again, I'm going to assume that you'll want to hoard your financial resources until an expenditure of this type is not a strain.

For the average new rep, the most practical and least expensive way to begin is to establish a sole proprietorship. This is the simplest form of business organization. *You* are the business, and the business has no existence apart from you. As a sole proprietor you report your income on Schedule C (Form 1040), which is then reported as income or loss on your individual income tax return (Form 1040). You can establish this type of business with little or no legal or financial help. Don't misunderstand—later on your attorney and CPA will become valuable allies in keeping the tax collector from confiscating the major portion of your earnings, but right now you'll fare much better by taking the easiest route.

Work from Your Home or an Office?

Over half the reps in business today work out of their homes. It's convenient, inexpensive, and practical—and I strongly advise against it. Why? Because it's not businesslike and gives a poor impression to both prospective principals and customers.

Suppose a desirable principal contacts you and wants to interview you for a line that has good existing business in the area. He may want to stop by your office and see how you operate. You have to lamely admit you're working out of the back bedroom and that you can meet in your living room or at his motel. This puts you on the defensive right from the start, especially when the principal compares you with your competitors who have convenient offices. Image is important. Working out of your home can cause your stock to drop faster than the Dow-Jones Industrials at the end of the summer rally. An office may seem to be a luxury, but it is actually a necessity. You can succeed working from your home, but you'll improve your odds tremendously if you rent an office and begin in a professional manner.

There are other drawbacks to working at home.

First, there is the question of self-discipline. If it's a problem for you, you'll find it easy to have that second cup of coffee, dawdle over the morning newspaper, or weed that small patch of petunias before running to the post office or making your first call.

Then there is the question of your wife—her interest, her availability. Some wives are completely caught up in the new venture and, if they don't actually help, they respect your need for concentration during working hours. But there are others who just don't identify with business and can't understand the need for total concentration or mundane paperwork. If you are around, you will be expected to baby-sit while she runs an errand, you'll be asked to hang around to let the TV repairman in. All these minor—and sometimes major—annoyances and distractions can be eliminated by renting your own office nearby and leaving home at the same time every morning.

Yes, this will be an added expense at a time when you need to watch every penny, but if you're resourceful it need not be a heavy drain on already tight finances. Some answering services (and you will need an answering service) have desk space available in their offices for a very modest fee. While this isn't the same as a private office, it has very definite advantages. You have a receptionist, and someone will always be there to handle an important call that may come in.

Even this budget option gives you a business address, and you can be a lot more confident when that important prospective principal calls. You can offer to meet him—for his convenience, of course—at his motel, or you can invite him to your office. If he prefers your office, you can explain your setup; he'll appreciate the fact that you have a real honest-to-goodness business address. When he arrives, if privacy isn't easily available, a nearby coffee shop will do. At least you've given a professional appearance by having an office away from home.

By checking with leasing agents you can often find a tenant in an unrelated business who has spare office space to rent out, usually on very attractive terms. Again, the rental can be adjusted to include the answering services of his or her receptionist. To negotiate the best price, you can point out to the tenant that you won't be receiving many calls for several months.

When beginning, either of these arrangements—space at an answering service or a sublease with another business—may be preferable to establishing your own office. It will cost you a lot less, and having someone to talk to occasionally, even if it's about the weather, can be comforting on those days when your sales calls don't bring the desired results. Paul Elkin started out this way, and it worked fine for him.

Remember, when you work from your home the only thing you save is the rent. You still have all your other expenses—phone, travel, insurance, and taxes. So, if at all possible, cut down somewhere else and use the money saved toward renting an office away from home.

A Honda or a Cadillac?

One of the largest expenses you'll have is your car. It will also be one of your most important assets. A dependable car is essential, and the type of car you buy should depend on the size of your territory. If you'll be working a metropolitan area with only a few out-of-town trips, you have an excellent opportunity to save on car expense. A small car, easy on gas and maneuverable, can be a real money-saver in your first years. Before you decide in favor of a foreign car, make sure you will have ready access to service and parts.

If you must make long trips, a small car might prove too fatiguing. For this event, the money you save on gas and operating costs can be lost if you are not at your best when trying to nail down that big order. A mid-size or larger car will make those long drives easier and keep you refreshed, and of course dealers in American cars are everywhere, even remote places.

The larger the car, the larger the insurance payment and the more gas you'll buy. For these reasons try to be realistic, and buy or lease the smallest car you'll be comfortable in for your particular situation. Later on, when the commissions come rolling in, the choice of a car can be left entirely to personal preference.

To lease or to buy is a constant question, and you'll not get a recommendation from me. Our agency owns one car and leases one, and frankly we're not sure which policy is best; nor are many accountants. If you do decide to lease—and the ramifications are many—make sure that you shop the field and talk to several companies, just as you would when buying a car. One caution when leasing: you may assume that the little extras, such as sales tax on the price of the car and license plates, are included in the monthly lease payment. This isn't always true; we got stuck for several hundred dollars more than we had anticipated when we leased our car.

When the time comes that you can afford a larger car, don't worry about its size as far as customers are concerned; they rarely resent being taken to lunch in a late-model luxury car. A sales manager or two, however, may cast an envying eye at your chariot; but that's a nice problem to have, and you can always explain that it helps on taxes.

Letterheads, Business Cards, and Paraphernalia

The purpose of this chapter is to prepare you to open and operate your rep business in the most economical fashion possible without sacrificing the professional appearance you'll need to attract principals and customers. Your business literature is vital to a good image, and an intelligent choice of letterhead and business card will go a long way toward creating an appearance of professionalism.

By all means, do not trot down to your hometown printer or local quick-style franchised shop and order a few hundred letterheads. The standard commercial printer will have to make up a special design and set type for your name, address, and phone number. Printers are not specialists in graphic design—they're printers. If you want something good looking, they (or you) will have to hire a commercial artist to design a letterhead, envelope, and business card—and it will cost you plenty.

An equally undesirable alternative is to have the quick-style printing store work up something. It will be cheaper, and it will look cheaper. Most of these franchised operations are run by people who haven't been in the printing business before, and their design capabilities are usually nonexistent. However they're great for other miscellaneous needs, as you'll see.

Happily, there is a good alternative to both the commercial printer and the quick-style printing store. Several excellent mail-order business products firms employ top-notch commercial artists to create attractive letterhead and envelope designs at modest prices. These companies can print thousands of each design in two or three colors at quite a savings because they need only one setup and one press run. When your order is received, they simply set your name and address (and logo if specified) in type and print an additional color on the design style of your choice. In this manner you receive attractive multicolor stationery and business cards at about one-half, or even one-fourth, of what a similar supply would cost from a commercial printer.

These companies buy quality bond paper in large quantities at extremely favorable prices, and part of this saving is passed on to you. For example, 500 letterheads, envelopes, and business cards currently cost approximately $70.

Two of the leading mail-order firms providing these services are The Drawing Board, P.O. Box 220505, Dallas, Texas 75262, and The Stationery House, 1000 Florida Ave., Hagerstown, Maryland 21740. Both firms will send you their catalogs illustrating the attractive personalized business forms they have in stock.

Later, as commissions increase, you'll have plenty of time to employ a commercial artist to create a personalized design for your agency.

The quick-style printing store is useful for printed forms other than letterheads. Every rep, for instance, should have a line sheet for his customers—a list of the principals he represents. This may change from month to month as you gain or lose principals; therefore, it's necessary at first to have an inexpensive method of printing this sheet. If you have a good electric typewriter, you can type up a presentable line sheet yourself. Then take it to the quick-style printing store; the operator will make an inexpensive paper master and print 100 copies for you for about $4 to $5, often while you wait. Add a little class by specifying black ink on colored paper. This will cost a few dollars more, but it will look much more prestigious.

Any other time you need a fast run of printed material where content and speed are more important than looks, visit your handy quick-style store; you'll save a lot of money.

Accountants and Attorneys

A good way to economize when starting up your business is to stay away from these two professional groups. Later they'll be worth their fees but not now, unless you're setting up in some business form other than a sole proprietorship. If you are, by all means consult an attorney and an accountant, preferably a CPA; but be prepared to shell out generous fees for incorporating or drawing up a partnership agreement and for setting up your financial records.

As a sole proprietor you can get along without professional advice for at least one year, maybe even two. Legally there's not much to do. You should write the IRS for an identification number for your tax return; at the end of the year your principals will request this number for filing their report No. 1099 with the IRS. This form, of which you'll receive a copy, will show the total commissions paid to you for the calendar year. Except for that, and filing a quarterly estimated income tax return which includes an automatic provision for your Social Security payments, there shouldn't be much need for legal advice in the early stages of your business.

As far as financial records are concerned, yours will be simple and easy to keep. You'll have no inventories and little capital equipment or other complicated entries that would require professional help. Most good office-supply stores carry complete record forms for almost any type of business.

You or your wife can easily learn to keep these records during the year. When it's time to prepare tax returns, buy an inexpensive instruction manual—both J. K. Lasser and H & R Block publish good editions—and follow instructions when filling out your return. The IRS also has a free publication titled *Tax Guide for Small Business.* It, too, is an excellent resource.

If commissions are a little better than you had expected, or if you simply feel you need help in working up your tax return, visit a local bookkeeping service, show them your records, and ask what they would charge to do your return. As an alternative, you might consult one of the professional preparers that are so prolific at tax return time, but use caution in your selection. In the past the government has expressed skepticism about the capabilities of some of these firms.

Buy Insurance

As soon as you cut the cord from your present employer, all your fringes cease. Don't wait for this to happen before buying insurance.

Before you leave your employer, replace those company insurance policies with personal insurance. Once you have left, you'll be so busy starting up your agency that you may put off getting this coverage, which could be disastrous. A sudden illness or accident could eat up much of the money you've saved for your business. Two essential types of coverage are life and hospitalization. Naturally, the more dependents you have, the more life insurance you need. The same is true of hospitalization insurance. Accident and disability coverage is also helpful, but you can't financially afford to cover all risks. It may be desirable to consider this additional coverage later when more funds are available.

If you turn to your local insurance agent, you will be shocked at the premiums you'll be asked to pay for the individual life and hospitalization coverage you need. There is an alternative—national associations frequently offer insurance coverage, and there are thousands of these organizations across the country. There's certainly one for almost every industry, and new members are welcome. In the metalworking industry, for instance, there are ASM (American Society for Metals), SME (Society of Manufacturing Engineers), and ASME (American Society of Mechanical Engineers), to name just a few.

Some associations for manufacturers' representatives also have comprehensive plans for their members. The group insurance plans available to members of many of these organizations are universally more attractive than individual coverage for two reasons: First, the cost is generally less, and second, your policy cannot normally be canceled unless the group policy is dropped by the insurance company.

Don't expect to obtain these policies at prices approximating the cost of your former employer's coverage since, in most cases, the employer subsidized a generous portion of the cost. In association group policies, nobody subsidizes the cost. Prices are slightly lower only because the selling of policies, the paperwork, and the processing of claims is cheaper for a group than it is when an individual is serviced.

My own life insurance policy is with an association. It not only gives me a reasonable fee for term insurance, but I've been refunded approximately 40 percent of my yearly premium because of the group's excellent experience factor.

Our hospitalization policy with the same association also covers our dependents, and we carry a $750 deductible per illness to keep premiums within reason. This protects us up to $15,000. It's relatively inexpensive to obtain additional major medical coverage up to $100,000, since most hospital stays are for less than three days. Through the high deductible, the insurance company is able to avoid paying claims on these two- to three-day stays.

Your only additional cost is that of membership in the association of your choice, which may be as low as $50 a year.

Join a Trade Association

Despite my warnings against unnecessary expenses, you should arrange to join a national manufacturers' representatives' association compatible with your field just as soon as you begin your agency. Many of these associations publish directories that are used by manufacturers in finding reps. The granddaddy of them all is MANA (Manufacturers & Agents National Association) of Irvine, California, with about 7,000 members at this writing, up from 1,700 in 1970. This is a national association serving all fields. MANA publishes yearly a 500-page directory; it generally requires a listing by January to assure inclusion in the directory, which is published in midsummer.

A listing of national groups follows. They will vary in size and effectiveness. There are also local and regional organizations that will boost your morale when you visit with fellow reps, but it's essential that you belong to a national group for nationwide exposure to potential principals. Here is a list of some of the more important associations. Most of these cover specific industry groups.

AGRICULTURAL & INDUSTRIAL MANUFACTURERS
REPRESENTATIVES ASSOCIATION
P.O. Box 1311
Mission, KS   66222

ASSOCIATION OF INDUSTRY
MANUFACTURERS/REPRESENTATIVES
   (for Plumbing, Heating, Cooling, and Piping)
250 Fulton Ave.
Hempstead, NY   11550

ELECTRONIC REPRESENTATIVES' ASSOCIATION
233 Erie St.
Chicago, IL   60611

HARDWARE AFFILIATED REPRESENTATIVES, INC.
Shepard-Benning Bldg.
St. Joseph, MI   49085

INCENTIVE MANUFACTURERS REPRESENTATIVES
ASSOCIATION
P.O. Box 1295
Danbury, CT   06810

INTERNATIONAL HOME FURNISHINGS
REPRESENTATIVES ASSOCIATION
666 Lake Shore Drive
Chicago, IL   60611

MANUFACTURERS & AGENTS NATIONAL
ASSOCIATION (MANA)
P.O. Box 16878
Irvine, CA   92713

MANUFACTURERS REPRESENTATIVES OF AMERICA
   (for Paper, Plastics, and Allied Products)
35 East Wacker Drive
Chicago, IL   60601

MARKETING AGENTS FOR FOOD SERVICE INDUSTRY
420 Lexington Ave., Suite 1712
New York, NY   10017

NATIONAL ASSOCIATION OF GENERAL MERCHANDISE
REPRESENTATIVES
111 East Wacker Drive
Chicago, IL   60601

NATIONAL ELECTRICAL MANUFACTURERS
REPRESENTATIVES ASSOCIATION
250 Fulton Ave.
Hempstead, NY   11550

NATIONAL FOOD BROKERS ASSOCIATION
The NFBA Building, 1916 M Street, N.W.
Washington, DC   20036

National Marine Representatives Association
401 N. Michigan Ave.
Chicago, IL   60611

The NAWCAS Guild
  (for Wholesale Apparel)
Suite 515
1819 Peachtree Rd., NE
Atlanta, GA   30309

Power Transmission Representatives Association
P.O. Box 1353
Shawnee Mission, KS   66222

Sporting Goods Agents Association
P.O. Box A
Morton Grove, IL   60053

10
THOSE ELUSIVE PRINCIPALS
How to Find Good Lines

TWO STATEMENTS that can be made about the rep–principal relationship without fear of contradiction are: it's difficult for reps to find good principals, and it's difficult for principals to find good reps. On the surface this seems paradoxical, but it really isn't. The problem is compatibility.

Two reps, equally gifted in selling ability, often achieve totally dissimilar results for the same company, but for no apparent reason. This dilemma has stumped experts on both sides of the desk for as long as the two groups have been working together. For this reason it would seem that once an effective team is created—a rep and a principal who complement each other and who together produce excellent results—it would take a bulldozer to tear them apart. Yet the relationship is frequently tenuous; a new sales manager or a change in a company's marketing philosophy can destroy an arrangement that might be considered a minor miracle by some observers of this singular style of selling.

Naturally, your concern as a new rep will be to find lines to represent. Don't make the mistake of thinking that almost any line will do initially, because poor or ill-matched lines can hurt rather than help you in your early efforts to become established. An old adage in the rep business, "You're only as good as your weakest line," means that a poor line can pull your other lines—the good ones—down to its level in the eyes of the buyer. Thus all the painstaking time and energy you've spent in finding good principals to represent can be wasted if you take on a company that has a bad reputation in three essential areas: competitive pricing, excellent service, and reliable deliveries.

I recognize that, as a beginner, you're not in a position to be too selective. You must obtain lines as quickly as possible and some, if not most, of those you attract will have definite shortcomings. Some of these shortcomings won't necessarily be a result of the companies' lack of desire for or poor attention to quality. More likely their apparent faults will be the result of a "poor marriage." They aren't the right lines for you in the first place, and you're not right for them.

A consolation may be that not only beginners suffer from this mismatch syndrome. Veteran reps and experienced sales managers make the same mistake. If they had or could find a magic formula for avoiding the occasional mismatch, they would both be willing to part with a fair amount of cash for the secret. However, good professionals on both sides tend to improve their records as they become more experienced.

Let's find out how to attract good lines as a beginning agent.

Of course, the ideal procedure for a new rep is to follow the example of Paul Elkin. By the time he actually opened his agency, he had five good lines. Paul didn't do this overnight. He planned well in advance and took his time. Also, as an employee receiving a monthly salary, he was careful not to recruit lines during daily working hours—a good pattern of action to follow for both moral and practical reasons. A prospective principal is looking for loyalty, among other qualities, and if he feels that you're taking advantage of your present employer he could be concerned about your taking advantage of him.

The ideal arrangement, then, is to have one or more lines to represent when you open your agency. This doesn't sound difficult, but it presents problems if you're taking a shotgun approach—sending out letters in volume to prospective principals. Several may reply at once, and you'll have little opportunity to check them out on short notice. If 10 or 12 respond, you'll be swamped and may find it hard to negotiate with them and still do justice to your employer.

The rifle approach—as opposed to the shotgun method—was used by Paul Elkin. It is usually much more successful for the long pull. Paul selected his targets carefully and went after them one by one. His personalized letter had a convincing ring to it, and his honest explanation of his employed status impressed potential principals with his ethical standards. Though he didn't sign up all the lines he went after, his percentage of hits was good and he was literally "in business" before he was in business.

The shotgun approach, however, has its merits, as evidenced in the experiences of both Dick Cole and Dan Jurgens. Dick needed lines immediately. He was in no position to write a few selected companies and then hope that he could pick up lines quickly. Instead, Sharon pounded out semipersonalized letters every day for several months and mailed them as soon as Dick signed them.

Dan Jurgens, though still employed, had the assurance of a maintenance income; thus he could afford to go for broke at any time. He also could employ a volume mailing method. While he didn't send out as many letters as Dick sent, he nevertheless covered almost all advertisers in *Surgical Business.* He immediately signed up two lines, and that was enough to encourage him to hang out his own shingle.

Apply the procedure that will work best for you. Each new rep has circumstances that will make one or the other approach practical.

Your Solicitation Letter

Put your best foot forward when writing to prospective principals. Many letters never elicit a reply because they're written on plain paper with the agency name typed in at the top. This conveys a lack of professionalism, which makes a bad impression. If there's one paramount piece of advice, it's the simple rule that says "Look like you're in business!"

The content of the letter should be heavily factual. Some agents send along a resume, but it's possible to tell too much and be disqualified on some minor point that may never come up in an interview. Prospective principals are interested in what you can do for *them.* So put yourself in their place, and try to imagine the advantages that you can offer. If you've sold in Colorado and Nebraska for years and are on a first-name basis with one hundred to two hundred purchasing people, say so. This kind of information is more valuable to a principal than the fact that you graduated with honors from the University of Colorado—which could even work against you with some sales managers, depending upon their educational backgrounds.

If you've won selling awards or moved quickly to the position of senior salesman, mention it. This will be more impressive than the announcement that you've decided to strike out on your own.

Common sense is the criterion, but here are a couple of sample letters that a new rep might send out. First, let's take the rifle approach.

H. A. Johnson, Sales Manager
Rock Royal Manufacturing Co.
2120 E. Woodland Blvd.
Lake Bluff, IL 60644

Dear Mr. Johnson:

In reviewing sales agencies in the greater Denver area that specialize in aluminum architectural products, I find none that represents your fine company.

Since you apparently are not represented here, I would like to introduce my agency, S. McCall Associates, with the purpose of having you consider appointing our agency as your representative.

At present I cover all of Colorado and three adjoining states—Kansas, Nebraska, and Wyoming. I've traveled this territory for ten years and have sold over $5 million worth of aluminum products during that period. My relationships with construction industry buyers and others utilizing your type of product is solid and current, and since I'm well acquainted with the fine reputation of your company I'm certain I could improve your sales here.

May I have the opportunity of an interview to tell you more about S. McCall Associates and learn more about your plans for the future in this area?

I'll be looking forward to your reply.

Yours very truly,

S. McCall

That letter could have been written by almost anyone—a veteran rep, a salesman who lost his job yesterday and decided to go into business today, or an employed salesman who's testing the water. Of course, in the last case the fellow may have to use a little more discretion if he's currently employed by one of the prospective principal's competitors.

The letter doesn't give any clue as to the age of the agency, yet it holds out a very attractive lure for the principal—a salesman experienced in selling the principal's product and one who has done it successfully. The letter is brief and to the point; there is time enough to be explicit about the current status of the writer after a reply has been received. This letter is individually typed and is sent personally to the sales manager or company president.

The shotgun letter, which follows, is printed except for the company name, which is typed in. The letter opens very impersonally.

Sales Manager
Rock Royal Manufacturing Co.
2120 E. Woodland Blvd.
Lake Bluff, IL 60644

Dear Sir:

The greater Denver area has experienced a tremendous growth over the past ten years, and the market for aluminum architectural products has expanded along with this trend.

I am interested in finding an aluminum architectural line to represent that will enable me to take advantage of my years of experience in selling to the buyers of this and other related products.

In reviewing the available literature on your company, I find your products to be quite compatible with those regularly sold to the construction industry, and I am wondering if you have considered representation in this area?

My personal selling goals over the past ten years have been realized, since I've sold over $5 million worth of aluminum building products and have an excellent following with buyers throughout the entire area.

May I have the opportunity of an interview to tell you more about S. McCall Associates and how I think we can sell your products in the Colorado, Nebraska, Kansas, and Wyoming area?

Yours very truly,

S. McCall

This letter is more general but still accomplishes most of the goals of the first letter, also without divulging the fact that the writer has a brand-new agency.

Both letters can be changed considerably depending upon the individual situation. If you've actually started your agency and have secured a line or two through a friend or business acquaintance, you can be more explicit and name one or two of your customers and principals, as well as include additional information that will give you a definite appearance of being established.

You have now trusted your letters to the postal service, and you anxiously peer into the mailbox for the next week or two hoping for—but not really expecting—an avalanche of replies from sales managers who didn't even know there was a market for their products in your area.

You'll receive a few perfunctory replies telling you they aren't interested or that you didn't research sufficiently, that they already have very capable reps in Denver. Still, you'll probably get a nibble or even an outright acceptance of your offer sans the interview. Within a week or two you may represent two or three firms. This is all very well, but you can't build a business on one or two lines. Let's therefore look at a few different methods of finding additional lines.

Want Ads and Display Advertising

Keep tabs on the classified section of your Sunday newspaper. This is not the best place for principals to advertise, but many of them do anyhow. The more sophisticated companies will place a display ad in the sports or business section where exposure will be heightened and their return is likely to be of higher quality. However, you can't judge from the size of the ad just how much potential a company has to offer. Even good prospective principals will skimp on their advertising budgets for reps.

Trade journals are another good source to investigate, and the product lines advertised will be in keeping with the journal's purpose. If you want to sell building products, where could you find a better contact than through a trade journal serving the building industry? These trade journals can usually be found at your local library.

There are several rep trade associations that publish monthly or quarterly journals, and these carry ads from manufacturers looking for reps. The monthly with the largest circulation is MANA's *Agency Sales Magazine.*

The Wall Street Journal has a classified section called The Mart, which features ads placed by manufacturers looking for reps. Look in the category called Business Connections. These ads, as well as those in your Sunday newspaper, cover all conceivable types of lines, so your chance of hitting on a compatible line for your agency will be less than if you stick to trade journals or association publications.

Also, there's nothing to prevent you from running ads in these publications, with the exception of the Sunday newspapers, which would not be productive. State your specialty, the geographic area covered, and the types of lines you're seeking. In the case of *The Wall Street Journal* and some trade journals, you can specify that your ad appear only in certain regional editions, where your most likely candidates will be located. This device saves money since you pay only for that regional edition and not for national coverage.

Other Reps

Established reps receive several letters a month from interested principals, but they have earned the right to be selective and so take on very few. Usually they have no objection to referring these lines to other reps, provided they don't represent competition.

If you know one or two reps, visit them and frankly state your case. You'll find them receptive, and when you become established perhaps you can do them a favor.

If you're fortunate, the first few companies you line up may conduct periodic sales meetings. This will give you an ideal opportunity to meet reps from across the country. Do as Paul Rice did and let them know you're looking for good, solid lines. Paul picked up several lines in this fashion shortly after his ill-fated partnership experience, and it helped him get back on his feet. In a situation like this, your fellow reps are usually quite willing to help you find lines inasmuch as you're established in a different territory and don't represent competition.

Trade Shows

Visit every trade show you possibly can that's related to the lines you have or want to obtain. Exhibiting companies are often in the market for new reps, so don't feel bashful about asking. I worked a booth for one of our principals at a three-day show where the company in the adjoining booth made a product compatible with our other lines. I automatically assumed the company had representation in our area and never once approached the company man working the booth. My sales manager—who was assisting me in the booth—did, however, and recommended our agency. We got together and worked out a suitable agreement.

An extra advantage to signing a contract with a firm that exhibits at trade shows is that leads are obtained as a result of the show, and you have the knowledge that you've hooked up with a company that's promotion minded.

Buyers and Purchasing Agents

If you are now an employed salesman and are personally acquainted with the purchasing personnel at a number of companies, let them know that you're thinking of going out on your own. Buyers are often asked by out-of-town sales managers to suggest prospective reps for their companies.

These same buyers are frequently aware of situations where reps are terminated. Ask your contacts in purchasing to keep you posted on any openings they hear of, and when these leads are passed on to you, get a letter off to the sales manager just as promptly as you can. Also, elicit as much information as possible from your purchasing go-between about your prospective principal. The more pertinent you are in your letter about the principal's capabilities, the more impressed the principal will be with your knowledge.

A Hard-Sell Letter

When you have one or two lines, you *are* established. In replying to ads or contacting prospective principals you've learned about from other sources, you can now afford to be much more aggressive. Here, for instance, is a letter our agency used when we were still aggressively seeking new principals.

> Sales Manager
> Rock Royal Manufacturing Co.
> 2120 E. Woodland Blvd.
> Lake Bluff, IL 60644

Dear Sir:

A few months ago we answered an advertisement similarly attractive to the one you placed here last Sunday. The sales manager who placed that ad, and who subsequently appointed us as his firm's representative, said he received 86 replies.

I'm sure that the response to your ad has surpassed this figure, which will present quite a challenge to you in trying to decide whom to appoint as your company's sales representative. I'd like to mention a few reasons why we think it will be worth your time to include Momentum Metals on your interviewing schedule:

> Our firm is young enough (3 years old) to be aggressive and old enough to have established some attractive accounts.

> We'll bet we make more new calls than the average representative organization.

> Although we started our business just prior to the recent recession, we've increased our billings throughout this difficult period.

> We're based in Dallas, which is the finest and most effective location for serving the major industrial areas of Texas and Oklahoma.

> Despite our relative newness, several top-quality firms have appointed us as their representatives.

> Our previous experience includes many years on

your side of the desk working with sales reps, and we think we know what you require in good-quality representation.

My partner and I are both former midwesterners who recognized the potential in the great Southwest, and today we're more enthusiastic than ever about the opportunities here.

We would appreciate the opportunity of an interview, at your office or ours, to tell you more about our capabilities.

Yours very truly,

Bill Krause

As you can see, this is a forceful, selling letter. We were trying to sell the prospective principal on our ability to do a job for him. Use this type of letter when you're 90 percent certain you really want the line. If you're somewhat doubtful, the letter can be softened; but it should still be strong enough to arouse the principal's interest to the point that you'll be given an interview. The interview, of course, is the key to your obtaining the line.

Whether you're still employed or have started your agency, there is certain essential knowledge you must acquire about additional prospective principals before you sign up. If you neglect discovering the answers to the following questions, you may waste months working for a company that simply isn't worth it.

Determining a Company's Capability

Here's what to look for in round two:

Is the company doing any business in your area now? This is important, not necessarily because you may inherit a few commissions, but because you'll get some assurance that the company can be competitive in your area. Many companies attempt to open up new marketing areas completely unaware that they are too far away to successfully compete with local firms. You may get plenty of inquiries from your customers when representing a firm like this, but unless it's a specialty item, orders will be few and far between.

Will you be one of the company's first reps? Never, under any condition, sign on with a firm that is new to the rep business. It has nothing to compare your results with and consequently expects too much. Such companies feel that your every selling moment should be on their behalf. The third rep a company appoints in your territory may work out—but almost never the first.

Is the company's product a common one? This partially duplicates the reasoning contained in the first question, but it's so important that it should be reemphasized. Local companies can be very competitive on certain items—cleaning chemicals, metal stampings, certain types of castings, and rubber goods, to name a few. This means that freight charges can kill you, plus the natural inclination of a buyer to try to purchase locally.

If you lived in Chicago and wanted to buy a Buick, wouldn't you pay a Chicago dealer a few extra dollars rather than buy in Milwaukee, 90 miles away, where warranty servicing would be an inconvenience? Of course you would. But if you were in the market for a $32,000 Finnish Fireball, and the only dealer in America was in Milwaukee, you wouldn't hesitate to buy it there. The same is true of some firms that try to market nationally. A Towson, Maryland, steel-casting firm will seldom be able to sell to the Texas market, because freight costs—which are considerably less for Texas suppliers—will rule it out. On the other hand, a specialty item made only by a company in the North would be a logical product line for a Texas rep to have, because he wouldn't be competing with local Texas manufacturers.

So check that product carefully, and determine if it has a fair chance of being sold competitively in your market.

Is the company reputable? This is harder to check out, but it's vital to your security. Some companies—few in number, fortunately—use reps to develop a group of customers. After a year or two these companies terminate their reps, try to hold on to the customers, and appoint new reps in each area to develop a new group of customers. If a previous rep was terminated, find out why. Call the old rep and ask for a frank explanation. We dropped a company that didn't measure up to our criteria of quality and performance and found that it had signed up Paul Rice. Paul wasn't aware of the difficulties and apparently didn't know we were the prior reps until after he had signed up. He lasted with them only a few months before he also dropped them. A frank discussion, had we both known the circumstances, would have saved him a lot of trouble and expense.

Check with a few customers to find out if they know of any good or bad experiences with your potential principals. You're playing for real now, and it's essential that the new principals you take on be reputable and capable of delivering on their promises.

Who's in charge? Here's a real puzzler. Somebody's in charge, and it's vital that you know who it is. Most often, of course, it's the sales manager, but in many smaller firms the president or owner still pulls all the strings. A good tip-off as to who makes the decisions is the behavior of the sales manager when he interviews you. If he narrows down the candidates and then tells you you're it, chances are the boss has given him the authority to do the job. On the other hand, if he goes back home without making a decision it can mean—although there are exceptions—he has to clear it with top management.

Of course, if the president comes out to do the interviewing, it definitely means he's running the entire show. In this event, you'd better pay attention or you're liable to be placing your trust and future with the company in the wrong hands. This means that, although the company has a sales manager, the president makes all the decisions. When a crisis arises, whether it concerns overdue commissions, poor product quality, or an aggressive competitor, you can't waste time discussing it with the sales manager. He doesn't have the authority to make a decision, so your best bet is to go direct to the president.

Again, it matters not who's in charge as long as you're able to recognize the ultimate authority when the chips are down.

What about the contract? Even if you're not a member of an agent's association, beg, borrow, steal—or buy—a specimen contract. MANA has one available for $10 to nonmembers, which will give you an idea of what is considered a reasonable contract. Unfortunately, the most important aspect, termination, is still governed by standards held over from the dark ages of rep–principal agreements. Thirty days is the magic number. Thirty days' termination notice was standard then and, for some principals, it's still standard.

Slowly but surely, through the enlightened efforts of parties on both sides of the issue, termination clauses are being revised. One common clause guarantees the agent commissions on orders received within a period of 30 days for each year of service to the company. If, for instance, an agent represented a company for five years, he would be entitled to five months' (150 days) termination notice. He would be paid commissions on all orders received during this period after notification of termination. Six months would be a practical maximum since the agent, by that time, would be anxious to find another company making the same or similar products to represent.

Established companies, recognizing that the rep incurs a considerable amount of up-front expenses, arrange for payment of commissions by the 15th of the month following shipment. Smaller companies, hard pressed for cash, frequently wait until they have been paid by the customer before making out a check for their agent's commission. If possible, obtain a copy of the contract before serious negotiations begin, since you may find your tenure with the company dependent upon quotas or other criteria that may not be wise or acceptable.

One company we'd been with for a few years suddenly decided to revise its contract to allow for termination if we didn't meet our sales quota for the year—a quota, incidentally, set by the company. This revised contract did nothing to improve our relationship with that principal, and we soon resigned the account. In this case, the company changed the rules of the game after we were considerably involved with it.

A poor contract, no matter how much you want the line, is bad news. Concentrate on working with companies that write fair contracts. A firm that issues a fair and straightforward contract usually follows the same philosophy in all its dealings. This makes an ideal principal.

Any advertising or promotional support? Most companies using reps are sadly deficient in this department. Their budgets usually cover a four-color brochure and an ad in the *Thomas Register of American Manufacturers.* That is normal and that's why they have reps. Further, it's impractical for most companies to do national advertising; a good program would bankrupt them and be of little value because of the nature of their products.

Specialty firms with perceptive managements usually make good use of their promotion budgets. If you're lucky enough to sign up a firm with this refreshing philosophy, hold on for dear life. Not only does it give you an introduction to potential new customers through sales leads engendered by the advertising, but often your other lines can benefit as well. After visiting a prospective customer on behalf of the principal doing the advertising, you'll find you have a new business acquaintance who can possibly use one of your other products. But do right by the principal who's putting out the advertising money—it comes first.

Any house accounts? House accounts are the bane of all reps and sometimes indicate the principal wants to have his cake and eat it too. He wants you to go out and spend your money scouting up new business but doesn't want to pay commissions on existing business in the area.

There are several exceptions to that rule. The company may wish to see how you perform before turning over a valuable account. Despite its conviction that you're the best candidate, your new principal may have invested a great amount of money and energy in developing certain accounts in your area. If the company agrees that, after a certain time and with proof of your effectiveness, it will award you the house accounts, then it is indicating good faith. On the other hand, a policy that stipulates certain customers will always remain as house accounts is bad news, and your suspicions should be aroused.

Another philosophy on house accounts is offered by some firms that make custom parts. It specifies that no commissions will be paid on certain parts made for house accounts, but that all newly designed parts you are able to sell to those house accounts will carry commissions. Under this arrangement, you're usually able to renegotiate commissions on the old parts at a later date—if you do a good job.

If any one of the alternatives to a strict house-account policy is followed by a prospective principal, you may have a pretty fair company to work for. Also, the fact that there is some existing business is extremely encouraging since it confirms that your new principal is able to successfully compete in your area.

Interview Time

You'll discover the answers to many of the previous questions during phone calls and correspondence with prospective principals. Hopefully, you'll also learn about the companies through personal interviews, though many companies still tend to appoint their reps by phone. Initially, you'll have to accept this modus operandi, because you need those first few lines. But it's a risky procedure. Principals who won't come into the area to interview you are giving advance notice of how important the territory is to them.

Once you're established, a personal interview becomes an essential you can demand. Our agency receives seven to ten solicitations a month from manufacturers seeking representation. Except for an occasional lapse on our part or in the case of a highly recommended company, we simply can't, and don't, take the chance of signing up sight unseen. Either the company comes to Texas or we go to Chicago, Cleveland, or wherever it is headquartered.

The interview is the time for absolute frankness and honesty. The outcome of this discussion can have a great impact on the future of your agency, and a lack of honest give and take can cost both you and the principal precious time and energy.

If the company is selling to an entirely different market than you are, make a courteous but firm departure. Don't try to save face by agreeing to an arrangement that is doomed to failure. If the principal sets quotas or starts out with other restrictive conditions designed to take up most of your time, don't sign; you owe most of your allegiance to your present principals who are paying you commissions.

Tell the prospective principal exactly how you operate—the type of customers you call on and your assessment of your chances to sell his product. All previous contacts and correspondence are meant to bring you to this point, and if the chemistry is right and compatibility seems assured, then agree to agree and get on with contract terms.

Your success in the agency business will largely depend on the quality of the companies you represent. The best salesman in the world can't sell the goods of inferior companies for long. Signing up with firms committed to excellence makes your job not only easier but also more fun. It's enjoyable to approach prospective customers knowing that your sales promises will be backed up by the companies you represent.

When a company constantly delivers what it promises, buyers are happy to deal with it. A reliable performance by a supplier on a continuous basis relieves buyers of some of their problems, and you'll be welcomed by your customers if you represent this type of firm.

An investigation of prospective principals is difficult and often time-consuming, but it can save you headaches later on. One agency in the mid-South will not take on a new principal without one of the partners actually visiting the company's plant and meeting its personnel. Further, it will not continue to represent firms that don't provide good service and that neglect to perform the necessary communication obligations and paperwork that will allow the agency to make the most of its efforts. This is a top agency, and its two partners produce $200,000 to $300,000 a month for their principals.

Not all of us can be this independent, but as we grow we can become more professional in our relationships and expect more efficiency and professionalism from our principals.

11
THAT FIRST YEAR
Key to Survival

IT'S OPENING DAY, and it's scary. You've cut all ties with your previous employer and are now an independent entrepreneur—the untried, untested owner of a manufacturers' representative agency. But if you have absorbed what you've read so far, you should feel fairly confident about the direction you'll take from here. This chapter will reinforce that confidence.

The first year is encouraging and discouraging at the same time. It's also bewildering and exciting. You'll wish you could look ahead and visualize your progress after a full year in the business. Perhaps you'll even daydream a little and compare yourself with the Elkins, the Byrnes, and the Mitchells. You will wonder whether you'll equal or surpass their first year's efforts. Fine, do look ahead; but do it on your own time—not your agency's—for you must now get to work.

News Release

As soon as you snare that first line, make some noises. Talk to the sales manager about a news release. If he agrees, write one and submit it for his approval. Here is a news release we used in 1977 that can serve as a model.

NEWS RELEASE

SOUTHWESTERN PRODUCTION SCREW MACHINE HOUSE APPOINTS MOMENTUM METALS

Dallas, December 15——Bob Donnelly, Vice-President of Marketing of Tulsa Screw Products Co., Inc., today announced the appointment of Momentum Metals of Dallas as exclusive sales representative for the company in Texas and Louisiana. "This association will assure a closer liaison between our Texas and Louisiana customers and Tulsa Screw," said Mr. Donnelly, "and we're pleased to have a professional sales agency like Momentum Metals representing us here."

Tulsa Screw, formerly a division of Braden Winch, is now an independent company serving manufacturing firms throughout the Southwest. The company is one of the largest of its kind in the Texas-Oklahoma-Louisiana area and operates over 50 Davenports and Brown & Sharp Automatics. In addition it has several automatic chuckers, 10 production milling machines, and a workforce of over 110 people.

Dave Braack, partner in Momentum Metals, noted that Tulsa Screw's capabilities are very compatible with the precision casting, forging, and powdered metal lines carried by his agency. He added, "My partner, Bill Krause, and I know that many of our customers will be pleased that we're now able to offer the products of such a fine company as Tulsa Screw."

Tulsa Screw is located at 2415 E. 13th Place, Tulsa, Oklahoma 74104, and Momentum Metals' offices are at 12803 Demetra, Dallas, Texas 75234.

Bob Donnelly, of Tulsa Screw, okayed our version and we had it printed at a cost of $6 for 200 copies. We sent the copies to Bob, along with our customer list, and he promptly mailed them out. We supplemented his mailing with one of our own to certain trade journals and newspapers. Local newspapers ordinarily ignore this sort of announcement, but if they have a "light" news day they often use practically every piece of public relations material received in the morning mail. Trade journals are more receptive. If you happen to have a trade journal or industrial newspaper in your marketing area, visit the editor or publisher and tell him about the new line. Current news is valuable to these editors and their reporters, and chances are they'll give you some space in their next issue.

You may also wonder about writing a news release heralding the beginning of your new agency. I have mixed emotions about this. From an ego standpoint, having your name and picture in the paper is great, but to prospective customers it advertises your status as a novice in the rep business and—regardless of your previous connections and obvious talents—bespeaks a venture that hasn't yet passed the acid test. It's better to drop in on customer acquaintances as an established rep, even though you may have opened your agency only a week or two prior to your visit.

Customer Notification

This operation is critically important in your first few months of business. It is vital that you inform your potential customers, most of whom will be acquaintances from previous business associations, of your new status as quickly as possible—even if you don't currently carry a line suited to their needs.

Your self-assurance in these initial visits may be crucial to future business relations with these customers. Review your past relationships and performances and, if you don't have a line that is useful to the customer, mention that you plan soon to add a company that will be a capable and competitive supplier for his needs.

If you do have a line or two that the customer can use, by all means solicit some business. But your first few weeks, or even months, should be given over primarily to making as many calls as you can to acquaint your business friends with your new agency. Of course, if you've been fortunate enough to obtain one or two lines with existing business in your territory, these companies should be visited immediately. And if some of them prove to be old customers of yours, so much the better. It creates immediate credibility.

After you've made that first visit, do something to remind the buyer or purchasing agent of your existence. Remember, "out of sight, out of mind" is truer in the rep business than any other. Buyers see salesmen all during the day and find it hard to remember who sells what. One of our good buyers, a man who purchases over a half million dollars of goods each year from three of our principals, remains unaware of three of our other lines despite my subtle but constant efforts to remind him. He has good suppliers for these other products and tends to put my companies out of his mind. It's still important that I continue to mention our lines from time to time, because if one of his suppliers disappoints him, he'll be seeking an alternative.

Even though you may have to burn the midnight oil, sit down about a week after each visit and write a letter to each buyer you've seen, detailing some feature of your lines that went unmentioned during your first visit.

To complete this first round, make a second visit after a reasonable interval to each buyer who showed some promise. If you've added another line by the time of your second visit, so much the better; you'll have something additional to talk about. Or this time, leave something with your name on it, as Paul Elkin did—anything to get them to remember you.

My purpose here is to impress you with the need to implant the name of your new firm in the mind of purchasing agents. A strong and unusual personality has an easier time of it, but only one out of twenty has this advantage and the rest of us must labor at the task. If you worked for a prominent firm prior to starting your agency and received better-than-average attention when calling on behalf of that company, you may have come to expect special treatment. You may find, however, that it was the company the buyers recognized and that, as an independent agent, the name Henry Atkinson Associates doesn't open too many doors—thus the emphasis on agency identification by one means or another.

Finding Additional Lines

During these early months your selling activities will be governed to a degree by the number of lines you have gathered. If you have several, you can immediately get about the business of selling, after you've performed the chore of acquainting all prospective customers with your agency's name. But if you're short of lines, the main emphasis must be on finding good-quality lines to represent.

If you've made your rounds twice and still have only one or two modest lines, it's time to pull out all stops and start a campaign to find additional firms to work for. You can follow Dick Cole's lead by saturating a certain industry (if you haven't already done so); or select leading candidates and pick up the phone, like Art Byrne, and tell the president or sales manager what you can do for them. Without strong additional lines, it's going to be tough to keep buyers interested in giving you an audience.

Of course, if you have two, preferably three, strong companies like a New England electronics rep I know, you may be kept busy just promoting and selling the products of those lines. This rep receives about the same amount of commissions from each company, and the total comes to a hefty figure. There are quite a few reps who are comfortable with this sort of situation, but most prefer a greater number of lines in order to spread the risk and minimize the damage a capricious sales manager could do.

Adding lines has another plus for all reps, regardless of how long they've been in business.

There will always be certain companies that can't—or won't—use what you're currently selling. When you add a line, some of these elusive buyers automatically become potential users of your new lines. What a pleasure to return to a purchasing agent's office with a product he or she can consider buying from you; it's even nicer when the purchasing agent is a friend who has wanted to buy from you in the past but couldn't because you had nothing to offer.

Yes, in many instances new lines—good sound ones, of course—can often lead to interesting developments affecting the success of your other lines. The more dependable lines your have, the better equipped you are to become an all-service sales agency to your better customers. Life gets easier when you find several customers beginning to depend upon you as much for your expertise and product knowledge as for what you can sell them.

It's a good idea to invite your customers to ask for help when a particular component isn't doing the job for them. You should have enough expertise to be able to define the problem, although you may need to call on one of your companies to provide the solution. This ability to help a customer also emphasizes the need to represent companies that are capable and willing to offer this service. The way to achieve that is by investigating prospective principals for these capabilities before agreeing to represent them.

Of course, as I've already pointed out, you probably can't be this particular in your first year. But each line—each good line—you take on strengthens your hand, and by the time you have several good principals you should be very selective when deciding which lines to accept and which to refuse.

A manufacturer reading this bit of advice could take offense since I'm recommending a thorough analysis of any company a rep decides to take on. But in my previous book, *How to Hire and Motivate Manufacturers' Representatives,* I gave the manufacturer the same advice about contracting with reps for their services.

Prepare for Principals' Inconsistencies

Just because you've snagged what you consider a prize principal or two, don't assume that all will be rosy from here on in. You'll be amazed at the variety of sales policies current at very successful companies, and you will have to be truly responsive and flexible if you're to present a solid, unruffled appearance to your customers.

One principal may be successful because it makes a product that comes up with zero defects, but the owner may be an independent character who will do business with certain favored customers only. A second principal may be extremely competitive in its product line but may take four to five weeks to quote. A third may do everything well as long as the sales manager—the president's cousin or son-in-law—stays out of the territory and doesn't annoy the customers. I could go on at length, but I'm sure you get the drift. These inconsistencies don't present insurmountable obstacles, but they are a challenge that, met with intelligence and good humor, can sharpen your selling skills and improve your ability to adapt to unusual situations.

Try to learn in the early stages of relationships exactly where your new principals' strengths lie. Unfortunately, the weaknesses often can't be anticipated, but they will surface soon enough. Companies frequently imply in their literature that they are tops at everything they do; they truly would like to be, but hardly ever are. A company may illustrate a complete line of electronic controls in its catalog, but it may manufacture only a portion of those illustrated, relying on perhaps as many as several other companies to private-brand the rest of the line. In a case like this, the principal may be very successful in marketing the controls it manufactures and carry the other controls as a service to its customers, as well as to fill out the line.

The new rep, unaware of the noncompetitiveness of certain of the principal's products, will aggressively attempt to market the whole line, only to have a sophisticated buyer point out that the rep's new principal can successfully compete only in the specialized portion of the line that it manufactures. This is embarrassing for the rep, but more often than not the situation arises because the sales manager of the new principal has chosen to ignore—or has forgotten to mention—that certain controls are not of his company's manufacture and are carried basically as a convenience.

There's simply no way you can eliminate these unwelcome surprises completely; however, once you've started representing a company, there are a number of things you should know before making your first call on its behalf. Here's an informal checklist of questions to put directly to the sales manager:

- What are your current delivery promises on each product in your line?
- Where do you find you're most competitive in terms of price and capability—and where are you least competitive?
- Have you had any quality-control or other problems in my territory and, if so, with which customers?
- How quickly are you able to quote on my customers' requirements?
- If a crisis arises and you're not available, whom should I contact?
- Will you provide technical aid for me in the field?
- Do you have a procedures manual outlining company policies on such items as terms of payment, handling of rejections, technical aid available, and other matters that may come up in day-to-day operations?

The answers to these and other related questions will give you a pretty good idea of what to expect when you actually start selling. But the answers themselves may not be as important as the manner in which they're given. If the sales manager is direct in his answers and elaborates on them, it's a good sign. But evasive or incomplete replies are early-warning signals that you're in for difficult times. This doesn't necessarily mean you don't have a good line to rep, but it does indicate that you should proceed cautiously in soliciting business until you've determined that the company really will come through for you.

Sales Reports

Sales managers collectively have one big complaint: They don't receive sufficient feedback from reps in the field. The more honest among them also admit they have the same problem with their own direct salesmen. Nevertheless, you can really endear yourself to a principal's sales manager by keeping him informed. Only the most regimented of them will insist on regular reports from their reps. The better sales executives simply like to hear from you when you have something important to tell them—how competitive the company looked on its latest quotations, what sort of acceptance a new product is generating in the field, or what the competition is doing. Communication of this nature proves to them that you're actively pursuing their interests.

You can devise forms for certain functions or order a supply from one of the several mail-order firms that specialize in providing them. True, written communications are time-consuming and your basic job is to sell. The good sales manager recognizes this, but by keeping him posted on current happenings you'll help him help you.

For example, the quotes of one of our firms were consistently high on a component for a good customer. I was finally able to wangle from the buyer the name of the successful competitor. I then told my principal's sales manager who the competitor was and about how high we were. Armed with my report, he convinced his quoting group to carefully analyze the next inquiry received from that customer. They did so and were able to make some manufacturing modifications that enabled us to win the next order. Without timely feedback we would have continued to lose business to that competitor.

Cold Calls

Cold calls can be discouraging. Most companies have well-established suppliers that they buy from regularly and have learned to depend on. If a buyer feels these suppliers are doing a good job, he or she will be reluctant to make a change. But every buyer has problems with some vendors, and if you keep making those calls, your persistence will pay off in inquiries and orders.

The eager but inexperienced rep goes about his cold calls in the wrong manner. Anxious to sell any of his lines, he usually drags them all out in front of the purchasing agent who is giving him valuable time. By displaying all of his wares at once, he dilutes the impact any one line might have and makes little impression on the prospective customer.

The logical approach is to present only one of your lines to a potential new customer. Naturally, choose the line that appears to have the most logical connection to the company you're seeking to sell. Concentrate all your efforts on that line, and you'll have better luck; you will be appealing to one need exclusively. Later, if and when you've been able to sell that particular line to the company, you can present the second most logical line and so on.

On the other hand, if the buyer has no need for the first line you present—and this may well be the case—you may as well take advantage of the fact that you have his or her attention and mention the products of your other lines. If you notice that the buyer pays particular attention to one of the products, then zero in on the advantages of that product.

This book isn't intended as a primer in salesmanship, but the selling strategies of the rep are decidedly different from those of the direct man, who represents one company and usually one product, or a few closely allied products. You have to be much more versatile than the company salesman and direct your sales presentation with a light and delicate touch. If you don't, you may oversell and thereby forfeit the initial impression you made on your customer. Remember, these procedures are for cold calls—calls on buyers and companies you've never contacted before. They naturally differ from the approaches explained earlier in the chapter that you will use with old friends and former buying acquaintances.

You should strategically intersperse cold call visits with visits to your regular customers to help you recharge your batteries. A visit to a current customer reinforces your confidence in your ability to sell.

Expenses

For the first year or two, and sometimes longer, you'll have to run pretty thin on expenses—but not too thin. You've got to keep up appearances, often more for the sake of your principals than for yourself. Your companies want to feel they're well represented in the field, and this means a first-rate agency. Sales managers don't expect impressive office suites; they want results. It's still important, however, to look the part of a successful rep.

Your traveling costs are inevitable, but in the early going you can save by putting up with something a little less opulent than top-of-the-line motel chains. If you look, you can find modest if somewhat inconvenient places in the cities and towns you visit. However, when you travel with your principals' visiting personnel, you must expect to stay at one of the better-known motels. These people are on company expense accounts and aren't overly concerned about a few extra dollars.

Your eating habits are your own, but modest-priced restaurants can still be found. With a little looking you can save several dollars a day by wisely choosing a reasonable restaurant.

With gas prices escalating, it stands to reason that you'll attempt to plan your trips very carefully. The less backtracking you do, the fewer miles you'll travel and the less gas you'll use. Scheduling car repairs can be tough, because Mondays and Fridays are your best days for this purpose; they are also the busiest days for auto mechanics. If you're in town tending to paperwork and yours is a multicar family, your wife or your children will surely be glad to lend you their car for a day. You'll find that you get better and quicker service from auto mechanics Tuesday through Thursday.

Chances are you won't use the telephone enough during the first years to take advantage of some of the newer services on the market. Several companies offer reduced long-distance rates, as much as 30 percent less than conventional charges, to certain cities across the country. There is, however, a minimum monthly charge that you'll have a hard time reaching unless you have several principals in these major cities. Good telephone practice can help keep your bills down. Watching time zones and rates applicable before 8:00 A.M. and after 5:00 P.M. can make a big difference. You can make calls before 8:00 A.M. to your eastern principals and at 5:01 P.M. to your California firms. It may mean getting to the office a few minutes earlier or staying a bit later on occasion, but that isn't a great sacrifice.

It goes without saying that there is no need for clerical help at this point unless you simply can't manage a typewriter. If you can't, take a quickie typing course, even if your maximum speed reaches only 30 words per minute. This will be much cheaper than hiring a secretarial service to pound out notes to principals and customers. When you have large amounts of clerical work to catch up on, hire a temporary or farm out typing to a service. Encourage principals and customers to correspond with each other directly, as long as you get copies of the correspondence from your principals. This means faster communication between principal and customer and fewer clerical duties for you. But do keep good customer files, or you'll find yourself uninformed. An uninformed salesman, obviously, isn't much help to anyone, including himself.

Don't worry too much about promotion and advertising costs, attorney and CPA fees, or other business luxuries at this point. These really aren't luxuries, of course; they will become essential services at a certain point in your growth. For now, except in unusual circumstances, you can do without them. In the next chapter we'll discuss how to find and make use of these services to your best advantage. Your current concern is reaching a good level of income; if you incur expenses that are not absolutely necessary, you'll find breakeven day receding further and further into the future. The first two years are really crucial. How you fare in this early period will set the tone for the future, so you must marshal all your energies and use them to the fullest.

There will be occasional setbacks; while these are normal for every business, they will be magnified in your eyes because you are just getting started. Try to attain a proper perspective in adjusting to early blows you may receive. If, for instance, a coveted line is awarded to someone else, just remember that there will always be other lines. There are over 300,000 manufacturing companies in our country. Most of them are small organizations, many using reps to sell their goods. In a year or two, if your name is in the proper directory and you have been doing a creditable job, you should receive a steady flow of inquiries from prospective principals. Our agency averages seven to ten a month with very little active solicitation on our part.

If you have followed my suggestions, had a little luck, and kept your mind on your goals, you'll find yourself gradually generating more and more business—which means more and more commissions—until you've reached breakeven day. This is a joyful time. It doesn't mean you can run out and buy a stable of racehorses, but it does mean you'll be able to breathe a little easier.

12
PROFESSIONAL SALES AGENCY MANAGEMENT
The Path to Financial Security

THE DAY HAS COME at last—you have finally arrived. Your monthly commissions are beginning to equal your business and living expenses, and orders on the books will bring commissions in excess of your budgeted needs. This may be one year or three years after you started your agency; regardless of when the day arrives, it's a cause for celebration.

At this point you can stop looking over your shoulder and begin looking ahead to the professional management of your agency's affairs. The more professional you become, the more successful you'll be, and the more good principals you will attract to your agency.

So far I have counseled a streamlined operation—no frills or fringes, only what's absolutely necessary. *Survival* was the password, and nothing mattered but the fundamentals that brought you to your present happy state. Now you should gradually reverse the procedure. As more funds become available, you should spend a portion on improving the efficiency and appearance of your business. To continue operating on a modest basis will retard the rate at which you grow, whether you choose to remain a one-man firm or bring several other people into your operation.

This doesn't mean you should go out and buy a Cadillac, install a WATS line, or move your office to a high-rise complex. What it does mean is a planned program of professionalism as funds become available. If you use all available aids, you'll have a stronger base from which to grow and prosper.

You can't hope to enlarge your agency without running it as every other successful business is run—on a professional basis. Let's review some of the steps that should be taken to move you from an emerging status to that of a first-rate agency.

Professional Services

By this time you may have engaged an attorney and an accountant. If you haven't, it's now important to do so.

If, as I suggested, you started out as a sole proprietorship, barring emergencies you have probably survived in good shape without professional services. However, with more money coming in, it's time to consider making a change in the form of your organization—a subject covered in a little more detail later in the chapter. Any change of this nature should be performed by an attorney, regardless of what the self-help books have to say on the subject.

You may soon be hiring employees, which will involve employment contracts, withholding taxes, and fringe benefits. An attorney will be needed to insure that all regulations are followed and that your interests are protected.

If you change your organizational form, your income tax returns will become more involved, and professional assistance will be required to make sure you pay enough—but not too much—to Uncle Sam.

It's important, then, for you to start looking for the best professionals you can afford, and a good place to begin is with the attorney. How do you locate the one who will do the best job for you? I don't have a foolproof answer, but I can give you some helpful suggestions.

The trouble in finding an attorney who will understand and help you with your problems is the lack of classification in this profession. If only it were as easy and clear as the medical field. Of course many lawyers do specialize and to some extent limit their practices. Some are expert divorce lawyers, others specialize in criminal law, and there are even a few who know what a manufacturers' representative is, but very few. Finding those few through regular channels is virtually impossible. Recent changes in the law permit attorneys to advertise, but this hasn't really improved the situation. Most ads list a wide variety of services and prices including drawing of wills, incorporating businesses, and helping with divorces and bankruptcies. These lawyers are obviously similar to general practitioners in medicine, not specialists in business law. How, then, do you find a lawyer who will be able to understand your business and give you good professional advice?

There are two ways. First, if you have a banker in whom you have confidence, ask him about attorneys he meets through the course of a business day. Bankers see all kinds, of course, but some, who are involved in business-related transactions, will be much more familiar to your banker than others and he'll have had an opportunity to judge their performance over the years.

Second, you can consult some of your peers, other manufacturers' representatives. Preferably, choose the owner of a firm with several sales people as opposed to an individual rep. He will certainly have made extensive use of an attorney by the time you visit him and should be a good judge of his attorney's value and effectiveness. In addition, an attorney who has been working with a rep won't have to go through the learning procedure that many of his or her associates will require, probably at your expense. Make sure, of course, that the agency's lawyer isn't just a needy in-law or cousin whom the owner is helping support.

If you're a member of MANA ask for its list of attorneys recommended by other members. After you've received several recommendations, visit two or three of the most likely candidates and ask some questions directly related to your personal interests. Find out if they have worked with reps before, if they're familiar with estate planning, and if they've ever been embroiled in contract litigation.

Also ask about their fees. The manner in which they respond will give you an idea of their capabilities. And don't overlook rapport. You must feel comfortable with the man or woman whose services you use; both parties do a better job when there's an easy compatibility between them.

How about a good accountant? This is a bit easier, because accountants are involved with more business-related functions than attorneys are. But it pays to find a good one, and here again it's not a bad idea to check with other reps of your acquaintance. The key question to ask is "Does your accountant ever make any tax-saving suggestions to you?" Many accountants or CPAs merely go through the motions of making the proper entries, filling out the necessary forms, and providing a quarterly or yearly statement. They seldom offer suggestions about how you can reduce your taxes.

Try, even if it takes extra time, to find a CPA who has a reputation for actively seeking out good tax-saving practices for his or her clients. It will probably cost you more, but it will be worth it.

Go over your needs with your prospective accountant or CPA and ask about fees. Have him include in his fee the cost for preparing your income tax return. Familiarity with your business makes your accountant the most logical choice for performing this task. Again, compatibility is important, for you should never hesitate to phone your accountant or lawyer when you have a question. That's what they're for. If you have rapport with these two advisers, you'll feel freer about contacting them.

Type of Organization

Although I recommended a sole proprietorship as the best form of organization when beginning your business, the time comes when you should talk to your attorney about changing to a corporate form—either a regular corporation or a Subchapter S form.

There are several good reasons for becoming a corporation:

1. If your personal taxes are getting into the upper brackets, you'll find the corporate rate lower.

2. Your personal liability is reduced. Make sure, however, that

this isn't the only reason you change, because the courts have allowed suits against corporate officers and directors personally. Nevertheless, there is a reduction in liability risk by going corporate.

3. A sole proprietor or a partner can put aside 15 percent of his income (tax-deferred) for retirement, but a corporate officer through a good pension and profit-sharing arrangement can deduct 25 percent of his income.

4. When you wish to sell part or all of your agency, it's much easier to sell stock in a corporation than to sell a portion of a business that is a sole proprietorship or a partnership.

The Subchapter S form has most of the benefits of a true corporation but allows you to be taxed as a sole proprietor or a partner. This can be good in some years and not so good in others, depending upon your total income. Normally this form of corporation is used to apply business losses against your personal income. It can also be used to spread profits among several people—members of a family, for instance—and generally saves money on taxes on profits.

Of course, when you change to a corporation, you become subject to much more control by the state and federal government. Frankly, it's considerably simpler from a paperwork point of view to remain a sole proprietorship. There are numerous pros and cons that you and your attorney must discuss before he or she can recommend which, if any, type of corporate form is best for you. Also, before visiting your attorney for such a discussion, read up on the subject. One book I can recommend is Marc Lane's *Legal Handbook for Small Business.** It not only explains this subject well but also covers many other legal aspects of running a small business.

Advertising and Promotion

Like the principals you represent, you'll find spending money on advertising and sales promotion one of the most difficult things to do. The car, the phone, and the rent are all very tangible expenses. It's much easier to write a check for these costs of doing business

*New York: AMACOM, 1977.

than it is to spend money on advertising or promotion. You simply can't measure what you're paying for, and so the inclination is to spend the least amount possible. Fortunately for you, most reps feel the same way; and if you stand out in this crowd by budgeting a reasonable figure for a good promotion program, you'll do exceptionally well.

Several areas are mandatory, and in some cases your principals may help out.

Advertising in the Yellow Pages can bring a rash of nuisance calls, similar to the leads you'll get from some of your principals that advertise in trade journals. But in both cases, a good screening of these results can bring out the gem or two worth pursuing. Our agency has received business for our principals amounting to several hundred thousand dollars through two customers that phoned as a result of our modest Yellow Pages ads. One of our principals co-ops with us; the others do not.

At this point you should also find a good commercial artist to design custom letterheads, envelopes, and business cards for your agency. You may even wish to have the artist develop a distinctive logo illustrating the type of lines you carry.

If your principals' products are suitable for trade shows, by all means get involved. This endeavor requries some expense, however, and before committing too much money, be sure the principals you wish to feature will bear the cost of the booth *and* send personnel to help man it. Occasionally it will be wise to share the cost. Once in a while you may have to spend some of your own money to convince a reluctant principal that exhibiting at a show can be profitable.

In 1976 we wanted one of our top companies to exhibit at a local show. The company hadn't had much success when its products had been included in a previous show with four or five other principals. However, we suggested that this time the booth be exclusively for this company and offered to pay the space cost of $100. All the company had to do was bring products and manpower. The company agreed; it exhibited, and within two weeks after the show we wrote an order for $70,000 attributable directly to a contact made at the show. Our commission of $3,500 represented an excellent return on investment.

One caution—trying to do too much at one show may have a negative effect; the prospective customer can be confused by too wide a variety of signs and products and lose sight of the one product he may be interested in. If possible, limit your booth to one principal at each show.

If you find trade shows work well for you, you'll want to build or buy your own exhibit. But these can be extremely costly and unwieldy. In addition, many exhibit centers charge exorbitant fees for transporting your exhibit from the loading dock to your booth location, often only a few hundred feet away. A number of companies make attractive standard lightweight exhibits that you can carry by hand.

Hiring Sales People

As your agency grows, you'll come to the day when it becomes impossible to expand further without additional personnel. At first, clerical aid can be a big help, relieving you of time-consuming paperwork. But you can be in just so many places at one time, and the hiring of additional sales people may become a necessity at some point. Of course, if you're happy at a certain level of income, as Dan Jurgens is, so be it; but take the same precautions Dan did—he notified his principals of his philosophy before he signed them up and at present has no pressure from them to add people.

Odds are, however, that your principals will expect you to continue increasing their sales in your territory; if you don't add people when necessary, they may pleasantly—or determinedly—suggest that you do so.

Your timing will depend a great deal upon your financial situation. If you're clearing $30,000 to $40,000 a year and getting used to it, it might be difficult to reduce that figure in order to fund a new salesman. At that point you really can't afford an extra person. However, choose a point at which you can live comfortably, and put all income over that figure aside for the day when you must add personnel. This isn't as easy to accomplish as it is for me to write—what with Uncle Sam's fondness for appropriating a large share of our incomes—but a sum of $10,000 to $20,000 can keep you solvent when a new salesman comes aboard.

One industry poll showed that agency owners seldom personally make more than one-man operations, but each agency owner still wants his agency to grow for several reasons—to keep his principals happy, to increase the value of his business for potential sale of the agency, to spread the risk in case of illness or disability, and for personal satisfaction.

How do you go about hiring a new salesperson? As I advised earlier on forming partnerships, it's probably unwise to hire a friend. Eventually you'll have to point out that you're the boss, and that may begin the dissolution of a friendship. If you have a capable son or daughter who shows a promising interest in your business, you may wish to take this route. Some previous work experience is mandatory; you don't want the heir apparent to look like an heir apparent to your principals and customers. Instead, he or she should appear as a capable salesperson, able to serve both parties efficiently.

In the absence of a son or daughter, likely candidates may be found among your former business associates. Many reps I know have hired salesmen whom they have personally worked with at one time or another. They have been confident of the person's capabilities, leaving very little to chance.

If none of these options are open to you, you can use the standard channels. Newspaper and trade journal classified ads are the most productive. One rep cautioned me once never to refer to *manufacturers' representatives* in ad copy because I might miss a talented potential salesman unfamiliar with the term.

Perhaps another danger in using *manufacturers' representative* is that you may attract a salesman who is only interested in learning the basics at your expense, after which he'll strike out on his own, perhaps taking a few of your lines along. This is an inherent risk faced by everyone in our business, and you'll have to face it too. It's still wise to minimize the risk wherever possible. Paul Rice worked for two different reps. He was let go by one agency and left the other of his own free will. He didn't take any lines along in either case, but that doesn't mean your sales people won't.

The matter of compensation is a confusing one, but it's vital to your agency's health, so let's evaluate several of the basic methods.

Straight salary. You'll find this method to be the most attractive to the largest number of potential employees—at first. It offers security and appeals to sales people who don't want to take the chances you did. After a while, however, they'll get somewhat impatient and feel they're also entitled to a percentage of the commissions from their areas.

Salary and commission. Here you offer a bit of incentive, and the man who comes on board on this basis probably has more self-confidence and is anxious to use his skills to increase his income.

Straight commission. The person who responds to this arrangement is a potential manufacturers' representative. He simply can't afford to go out on his own and will come to work for you if you'll turn over the existing business in his territory, and you should. Also, the commissions from that business must be sufficient for him to live on, at least modestly. By agreeing to this arrangement, he's banking on his ability to make a good income through his selling skills. He'll probably make a very good salesman. Incidentally, his share of gross commissions should range from 60 to 70 percent.

On the straight-salary and salary-plus-commission basis, you generally pick up all expenses. The straight-commission man will usually pay all his own expenses.

These are the three basic pay plans used by most agencies. But they are just that—basic. You'll find any number of variations on these plans including quarterly or annual profit-sharing arrangements, retirement plans, and other fringes. Almost every agency owner applies his own special touch, which is often dictated by individual circumstances, such as the case of a salesman saddled with a large territory with little potential. He must be compensated differently than a salesman for the same firm serving a dense industrial area.

Before arranging any type of compensation plan, visit three or four other reps in your area who have employees. You'll find many of them began with one plan and switched to another because of local conditions or difficulty in keeping good people. Analyze their systems in light of your own agency—its lines and the territories that will need coverage.

There's simply no way to recommend one system over another. It's what fits best for you. But do as much preparatory work as possible before signing up your first salesman.

When hiring sales people under any system, consider strongly the advisability of drawing up an employment contract. A well-drawn contract can minimize the chances of your salesmen leaving and taking lines with them, or of their joining a competing agency and using knowledge gained at your expense.

These contracts are more enforceable in some states than in others, but regardless of their legal clout, they tend to act as a deterrent. Your attorney will be familiar with local conditions, and you should rely on him or her to write a contract that takes into consideration your individual situation.

And while we're on the subject of salesmen, let me add that the term *salesman* is used only for convenience. Numerous agencies have found women to be valuable additions to their sales staffs. One eastern agency owner had business transactions with a woman in a customer's plant and learned that she had asked several times for a transfer to the company's sales department without success and had finally left the firm out of frustration. The agency owner, whose firm handled electronic components, had been impressed with the woman's knowledge of the electronic-component business and offered her a job with his agency. At last report she was bringing in approximately $2 million of gross sales per year and still climbing.

Trade Association Activity

Initially you will have joined a trade association of manufacturers' representatives because it can be of help to you in getting lines, but this is only the tip of the iceberg. A good association will benefit you in many other ways.

I'm a member of MANA (Manufacturers & Agents National Association), as are the six men whose agency beginnings we explored earlier in the book. By way of example, I'd like to tell you how belonging to a good association like MANA can be a boon to your business. (There are many fine trade associations, some of which were listed in Chapter 9, but MANA is the most comprehensive, covering all reps, regardless of the industry they serve. That is why it is discussed in such detail here.)

MANA's monthly publication, *Agency Sales Magazine,* runs about 50 pages per issue. The editorial content is excellent, describing the latest techniques employed by reps across the country. Experts from other fields also advise on a variety of topics vital to our business. There are, for instance, articles by lawyers about contracts and contract termination. Almost every month, MANA's own CPA writes about taxes, bookkeeping procedures, and the sale of a business, and he offers pertinent comments on possible audits by the IRS. These articles are personalized for the rep trade and are thus relevant to the everyday conduct of our business.

Also included in the pages of *Agency Sales Magazine* are advertisements by principals looking for reps. Another classification offers space for reps to advertise their availability to prospective principals.

Through its commission arbitration system, MANA is often able to arrange for the settlement of disputed commissions that are overdue or that are being ignored. With 7,000 members behind it, the association carries some influence when attempting to provide this service, and it has been successful in collecting well over a half million dollars in overdue commissions for its members over the past five years.

There is also a "warn" file that is available to both reps and principals. If a rep feels he has been treated unfairly, or a principal thinks a rep performed unethically, either can write MANA and register a complaint. This is kept on file, and when a rep inquires about a prospective principal or a principal about a rep, the inquiring party is referred to the complaining party and can then judge the validity of the complaint firsthand. I should mention that this service is available to members only. You may therefore wonder why I've included principals. MANA welcomes principals as associate members at the same dues reps pay. In the last few years the association has paid increasing attention to associate members and now conducts a full-blown program for them, including seminars and a monthly newsletter.

Jim Gibbons, a former agent and president of MANA, has long believed that the association should work toward achieving a solid relationship between both parties, since each is totally dependent upon the effectiveness of the other. To do otherwise or to act as a *rep union* would be self-defeating; his philosophy is working well.

MANA holds approximately four seminars a year in different parts of the country, varying the locations each year so that practically all its members will be within commuting distance of at least one seminar over a two-year period. These two-day sessions are divided into two programs. The first day is for principals only, and MANA helps them discover how to work with reps for profit.

The second day is for reps only and covers all aspects of running an efficient agency. This session always lasts well into the evening, but the participants leave the seminar well satisfied with the results of the day, judging from the comments the staff receives personally and by letter. Both seminars are conducted on a freewheeling basis with questions from the floor encouraged. Many of the participants offer answers to their peers' questions and thus the benefit is twofold.

Once a year MANA publishes a directory of all members categorized alphabetically, by territory, and by product lines. This 500-page directory is used by 25,000 manufacturers each year when searching for new reps.

One of the most helpful aids to a rep member is the collection of reprint bulletins available from previous issues of *Agency Sales Magazine*. As you can see from this selected list of reprints currently available, these represent a specialized library on almost every subject of interest to a rep.

Stock, Profit-Sharing Plan, or Pension Retirement Plan for Agency Associates?

A Countdown on the Rising Cost of a Sales Call
What's a Fair Commission Rate Today?
Commission Reduction on a Negotiated Bid
Stop Hustling, Start Planning
"Performance Is Our Only Excuse for Existence"
How to Improve Your Image: "Mirror, Mirror"
Liability Insurance
Case Studies in Multi-Man Agency Operations
A Business Buddy: How Do You Stop Him from Becoming a Competitor?
Does That Line Pay a Profit?
16 Ways to Sell Engineering Departments
How Can a New Sales Rep Get an Established Line?
Cost Analysis for Manufacturers' Representatives
Agency's Questionnaire Digs Out Facts on Prospective Principals
Planning in a Manufacturers' Agency
Contract Between an Agent and His Sales Employee
An Employee Contract
Should Manufacturers' Agents Engage in Market Research?
Direct Mail for Manufacturers' Agents
Collecting Commissions: Learn about Your Legal Rights
Incorporation for Sales Reps
The Multi-Man Agency
Product Liability
Organize Your Office
How to Maintain the Balance Between Agent and Principal
Communications Is the Name of the Game
It's Time to Look at Your Agency-Manufacturer Agreement
Things a Representative Owes to His Principal
How Should Agents Be Paid When Pioneering a New Product?
Survey of Commission Rates
How Do Manufacturers Work Out Split Commission Arrangements?
Know Your Contracts
Termination of Agency Contracts
Covenant Not to Compete Must Pass Strict Tests
Contracts: The Making and Breaking of a Promise
Communicate for Success

MANA also offers several insurance programs, sample contracts, a guide for territory assignments (see MANA's territorial map on the opposite page), a list of attorneys and accountants familiar with rep procedures, special rates for auto renting and leasing, and a host of other advantages.

Probably the most important element membership in such an association can offer is the assurance that "you are not alone." As an independent agent you'll often feel isolated, and with good reason. You chose to enter what can be a lonely business, providing little contact with other members of your profession. A representatives' association fills this void and gives you a rallying point to turn to in both the good times and the tough times.

Delegation

An active agency owner is a secure one. When an owner becomes lazy and spends more time fishing than working, he's ripe for a raid on his lines by observant opportunists. Principals may be located in far-off cities, but they can tell when your personal activity has slowed down. That's when they become receptive to other approaches.

By remaining active, I don't mean that you have to be out selling more than ever; you may not have to sell at all. But you should be extremely close to the action as an administrator. Know exactly how each of your salesmen is performing, make frequent trips with them to the territories, and keep in close touch with your customers and principals. In this manner you'll maintain close control over your agency's progress.

If you decide you've got a great group of salesmen out there making money for you and that you're going to take it easy, you're in for a surprise. A rudderless ship drifts, and the crew often becomes uneasy and disturbed, particularly if it's a good crew. Soon the members of the crew—your sales team—will sense the lack of leadership and will probably do something about it. They'll band together; and since they're now probably on better terms with your principals than you are, they will have a fair amount of success in setting up their own new agency with your principals as their main-

Typical Marketing Areas

1. Eastern Massachusetts, Rhode Island, New Hampshire, Maine.
2. Connecticut, western Massachusetts, Vermont.
3. New York City, Long Island, Westchester County, New Jersey north of Trenton.
4. New York Upstate.
5. New Jersey, Trenton and south, Pennsylvania east of Harrisburg.
6. Maryland, Delaware, District of Columbia, northern Virginia.
7. Southern Virginia, North Carolina, South Carolina, eastern Tennessee.
8. Georgia and Alabama.
9. Florida.
10. Western Pennsylvania to Harrisburg, West Virginia.
11. Ohio north of Route 40.
12. Ohio south of Route 40, Kentucky.
13. Indiana except northwestern counties.
14. Michigan and Toledo, Ohio.
15. Illinois, north of Rt. 36 and Lake, Porter and LaPorte counties of Indiana.
16. Wisconsin and Northwestern Michigan (area northwest of Lake Michigan).
17. Minnesota. May include North and South Dakota and all or part of Iowa and Nebraska.
18. Eastern Missouri, southern Illinois.
19. Western Missouri, Kansas.
20. Louisiana, Mississippi, Arkansas, western Tennessee.
21. Texas and Oklahoma.
22. Colorado, Utah. May include Montana, Idaho, Wyoming.
23. California, Bakersfield and south, Arizona, Southern Nevada and New Mexico.
24. California, north of Bakersfield, part of Nevada.
25. Washington and Oregon.
26. Alaska.
27. Hawaii and Guam
28. Puerto Rico and Caribbean
29. Eastern Canada.
30. Western Canada.

OTHER TERRITORIES

31. INTERNATIONAL
32. NATIONAL
33. MEXICO & CENTRAL AMERICA
34. SOUTH AMERICA
35. EUROPE
36. ASIA
37. MIDDLE EAST
38. CONTINENTAL U.S.

© Manufacturers & Agents National Association

These territorial designations are only suggestions, and should be modified to suit your needs and the marketing capabilities of your manufacturers' agent. The modifications should be based on the type of material or product to be sold, your agent's established territory, natural geographic boundaries, and historical marketing divisions. The agreed upon territory or territories should be included in the contract with your manufacturers' agent.

stay. It has happened many times in the past and will happen again.

By remaining an active leader, you can head off such attacks at the pass. Should one of your employees solicit one of your lines to set himself up in business, which can happen even if you are active, don't play around; take prompt dismissal action. You've worked too hard and too long to be helpful to a potential new competitor.

Fortunately, most agency owners remember their struggle to become successful and they work hard to maintain a viable, productive agency. They hire good people and stay in control through constant attention to business.

When the day comes that you want to take it easy, it's time to sell your agency. We'll cover this interesting possibility in the next chapter.

A Word about Principals

You may have deduced from earlier sections of this book that the relations between principals and reps are "them against us." In the early stages of your business, this will appear to be true. For an unfathomable reason, some companies simply haven't learned how to run a progressive rep sales program. Some of these problems are attributable to very small firms headed by entrepreneurs, similar to you. They're as independent as you are and often unwilling to compromise. Either you do it their way or you don't do it. These are the firms that will be seeking out younger rep agencies, generally because veteran agencies long ago stopped representing them.

However, as your agency grows and you become more established, you'll find a welcome trend developing. There are many truly professional principals out there, and they're working with the professional reps. Within these two groups, relationships of many years' standing are the rule rather than the exception. Our agency—now in its tenth year—has good, solid companies to represent, most of them having had rep sales programs for 15 or 20 years and some much longer. For them to have worked with reps for this length of time, they have to be doing something right—and they are.

Communication is usually at the core of a good rep program. A first-rate principal keeps you well informed about everything that's going on in your territory. You receive copies of quotes, order acknowledgments and changes, invoices, and all correspondence. This information makes you more effective in the field—and the wise principal provides communication on a continuous basis.

You must reciprocate, however, if you expect the principal to be satisfied with your services. Communication cannot be a one-way street. Most companies don't expect call reports but want to be informed of anything important going on in the field. Usually they won't assign quotas, but they may reasonably expect a forecast of some sort. This is in your best interest, since it helps you discover what your customers are planning for the coming year. Keep good principals informed, and they will keep you informed.

Since professional reps are in short supply, you'll find that principals are eager to learn how to work better with their reps in order to attract and keep good professionals. Their membership in MANA has increased dramatically, and seminars for principals are almost always booked to capacity.

This can only be good news for manufacturers' representatives. A growing interest in improving their rep sales programs means more sales for those principals who pursue this course and more commissions for their reps. If you can gradually work toward representing a group of companies that have this desire to excel, happy days are ahead for you.

13
LOOKING AHEAD
The Future Can
Be Exciting

THINGS ARE HUMMING along. Commissions are increasing and everything is right with the world. So now it's time to look down the road.

"Look down the road? After three years of struggling to make ends meet, I'm just now starting to breathe easy, and you want me to look down the road? Incredible!"

That's right, because now the good part comes. After all, that struggle you speak of has to be worth more than a big house, a nice car, and $50 in the bank. And it can be. It can mean a comfortable early retirement or—for you eager beavers who may tire of selling and look for other fields to conquer—a chance to start or invest in another business or two. To quickly gain your attention, let me back up my contention by showing you a table illustrating what a yearly $7,500 investment in a Keogh retirement plan can do for you by the time you're 65. And if that's too long to wait, you can begin taking your funds out at age 59½. This table is based on 8 percent compounded annually.

Beginning Age	Total Accrued at Age 65
30	$1,292,370
35	849,622
40	548,287
45	343,207
50	203,640

And these figures don't even take into account the amount you can put away if you incorporate your business. A corporate plan has a much larger maximum that can be saved, tax-deferred.

If you launch a good retirement program as early as possible, it will mean that when and if you sell your business the receipts from that sale will be an extra bonus with which you can buy that ranch or cruiser you've always wanted.

It's easy to put off thinking about these future benefits because the payoff is a number of years away; but the longer you wait, the smaller the pot at the end of the rainbow. I can't urge you strongly enough to start planning just as early as possible—even sooner. If you don't, you may not be able to retire because of insufficient funds to keep you going; worse, you may lose several of your lines to younger agencies. This compounds your problem because your agency will have no market value.

In this chapter we'll discuss retirement plans and the sale of your business. It's never too early to think about both programs.

Recognizing that each person must decide how much he can put away toward later comforts, and also noting that Congress is constantly changing the rules of the game, let's look at the various options you have now or will have later as your agency grows.

IRA (Individual Retirement Account)

Before you consider any type of program, experts recommend that you reserve a backup of ready cash that will enable you to run your business and pay living expenses for at least six months, preferably an entire year. These funds should *not* be in a retirement fund, since removal of money from such a fund is difficult at best and, when withdrawn, is often subject to a tax penalty.

Assuming that you have made this provision and your personal income is now at $15,000 to $20,000 a year, you'll want to look at the possibilities of an IRA account.

Basically, this plan allows you to put away up to 15 percent or $1,500, whichever is less, tax-deferred. In other words, if your taxable income is $20,000 and you put $1,500 (the maximum allowable) into an IRA account, your taxable income drops to $18,500. In addition to this, all the interest, income, or capital gains realized in this account compound over the years, tax-deferred. When you begin to use this money at age 59½ or later, you are taxed on the basis of your yearly total income at that time, which normally would be lower than during your peak-earning years.

If your wife helps you in the business or works elsewhere and is not covered by another pension plan, you can take out an IRA plan for her also.

This plan is essentially handled through banks and savings and loan organizations in the form of savings accounts or CDs (certificates of deposit) and will compound at interest rates available from those institutions. The IRA plan has its primary usefulness in your first few years, if only for the purpose of getting you into the habit of putting a portion of your funds away for the future. Its use as a long-term vehicle for retirement funds is limited because of the $1,500 yearly maximum. When you substitute a more sophisticated plan for your IRA, your original funds will remain in the IRA account—compounding gains, tax-deferred. As a rule, they cannot be transferred to another type of fund.

The Keogh Plan

Here we have a much more attractive, flexible retirement fund, available to sole proprietorships and partnerships. As soon as your income starts inching upward, you should begin thinking about initiating a Keogh fund. The yearly maximum is 15 percent, or $7,500 of your taxable income, whichever is less.

Depending on the plan, you can put your money into all kinds of investment instruments—stocks, mutual funds, savings bonds, CDs, gold stocks, annuities, coins, stamps, even real estate. Again, the compounded gains over the years are tax-deferred until you begin to draw them out.

A few of these Keogh investment opportunities are worth further explanation.

Mutual funds. Each mutual fund will have its own plan, and if you join one of these plans you must adhere to its regulations. One of the best types of mutual funds has several different funds within its organization. These companies may have an income-producing fund, a blue-chip stock fund, a conservative bond fund, and a speculative fund. You will probably be allowed to move your invested money from fund to fund, even by telephone, in order to take advantage of varying economic conditions.

If the stock market is rising, for instance, you may wish to switch from an income-producing fund to a blue-chip or speculative fund. This can be done without penalty at any time. However, you are stuck within the framework of the parent fund and cannot invest in other opportunities outside that fund's provisions. One other note about mutual funds—some levy a sales charge that can go as high as 8 percent, merely for the privilege of investing in the fund. Studies of the long-term results of load funds (those that levy a sales charge) and no-load funds (those with *no* sales charge) do not show an appreciable difference. Therefore, the no-load funds appear to be a better bargain.

Every August *Forbes* magazine publishes a detailed report on mutual funds to show how each fund has performed over recent years. By all means read this report because once you've put your money into a mutual fund it's a great deal of trouble to change.

Savings institutions and commercial banks. Most of these organizations have relatively unsophisticated plans. They customarily recommend either savings accounts or CDs, and your funds will compound at conventional interest rates with no opportunity for capital gains.

Some commercial banks—those with trust departments—may have collective funds similar to the mutual funds mentioned earlier. These plans also offer the option of moving money from one fund to another. However, since bankers are not normally risk-takers, their collective funds are not known for magnificent performance. The mutual funds, on the other hand, must perform in order to stay alive. So if you like the idea of collective funds, you may wish to closely review the performance results of mutual funds versus banks before investing.

Insurance. If you've ever shopped insurance rates and policies, you almost certainly wound up very confused and fell back on the advice of the insurance salesman or agent who made the best impression. Personally, I'd rather place my retirement plans on more substantial ground.

Insurance companies have a plethora of plans, some involving life insurance and others annuities. I know from personal friends that the retirement-fund market is an excellent one for insurance sales people; therefore, the profit must be lucrative. This profit naturally is extracted from the customer. The fine print in insurance contracts is usually couched in language not easily comprehensible to laymen—a fact that always makes me uncomfortable when loosening my purse strings.

For this reason, and because of my general wariness of the insurance industry, I won't even try to explain the various insurance plans. Try to find someone knowledgeable and experienced in such matters. However, if you feel you have the sophistication to intelligently analyze an insurance retirement plan, you should review it in comparison with other investment opportunities available.

The self-directed plan. Here is a plan that offers the participant an excellent opportunity to use his retirement money for a wide variety of profitable investments. Unfortunately, banks and other investment institutions offering this type of plan are scarce. Usually, banks look upon Keogh plans as a necessary nuisance because of the $7,500 yearly maximum contribution and keep their plans as simple as possible. But some banks realize that with tax-deferred compounded interest and capital gains, these modest accounts can often grow to $200,000 or $300,000 within 15 or 20 years. Since the bank's yearly fee is a percentage of the assets in each fund, this can result in attractive business for them.

The self-directed plan means that the individual fund investor can personally direct the regular investment of all of the funds in his Keogh plan at any time.

For instance, you can call your bank contact and ask him to take some of your money out of a mutual fund and invest it in gold or silver, or even gold coins. A month or two later, or a year later, after the gold or silver has hopefully risen in value, you can instruct him to sell it, put the proceeds back into your account—tax-deferred— and leave it there (where it collects compounded interest, also tax-deferred) until you decide to invest it elsewhere.

The important advantage is that you aren't locked into one type of investment. Through your broker and the plan, you can invest in any one stock on the listed exchanges, sell it, and put all or part of the proceeds in a six-month treasury bill—or church bonds, if you wish. You can even invest in real estate, but there are restrictions here since, according to the government's conditions for the Keogh plan, you have to pay for the entire piece of property; you can't make a down payment and owe the balance.

The self-directed plan offers a chance to vastly increase the value of your retirement funds. There is a documented case of a doctor on the West Coast who parlayed a $2,500 Keogh investment into a gain of almost $200,000 within two years by investing in a "hot" stock. The gain was tax-deferred. Of course, the doctor may have had other income sufficient to allow him to take this flier with his retirement funds, whereas the average person who depends on these funds for a comfortable old age might consider this type of specula-tion foolish and would probably be discouraged by a bank trust of-ficer. Nevertheless, it remains true that rewards from your own self-directed fund can be considerably greater than a savings ac-count or CD-type investment.

The self-directed plan is not for everyone, however. If you be-come nervous when the value of one of your common stocks drops a dollar or two, perhaps you should think of investing directly in a conservative bond mutual fund where the value changes little but an attractive interest rate is earned. Of course, you can also make this type of investment through a self-directed Keogh plan, but you'll be paying the bank a fee for maintaining it in addition to the management fee the mutual fund charges.

When seeking out the type of Keogh plan I've just described, ask your banker if the bank has a self-directed plan. He or she may mistakenly say yes if the bank has several collective funds whereby you may direct the moving of money from one fund to another, but that's not a true self-directed plan. You'll have to go one step further. Ask your banker whether you can purchase individual stocks or bonds through an approved arrangement with your broker or make other individual investments through the plan. The banker's answer will then tell you if that bank has a self-directed plan. If you cannot make other investments outside the bank's collective funds, then the bank does not operate a true self-directed plan.

It may be hard for you to find a bank with a self-directed plan in your area, but most banks that offer these plans—such as the Lakewood Bank and Trust Company in Dallas—are legally permitted to handle out-of-state Keogh accounts.

The government imposes several other conditions on Keogh-plan participants. If you have employees, you must contribute to the plan on their behalf at the same percentage rate you contribute for yourself. If, for instance, you decide to contribute 10 percent of next year's earned income to your plan, you must also contribute 10 percent of the earned income made that year by each of your employees. However, an employee is not required to be a participant in your plan until he or she has worked for you at least three years. You can include them at any time before the three years if you wish. Part-time employees working fewer than 20 hours a week need not be included at all. There is only one problem connected with covering employees under a plan, whether Keogh or corporate: If you don't invest wisely and the employees' share of the plan decreases or doesn't increase at a reasonable rate, the employees can bring suit against you for mismanagement of the plan. If employees are covered under your plan, it's wise to pursue a fairly conservative investment policy or let them manage their own account.

The only income upon which you can base your Keogh deduction is your *earned* income. Your salary and any profit your agency makes that is reported by you is earned income. So is any remuneration you may receive as a result of other self-employed endeavors such as writing, consulting, and speechmaking. Dividends and interest from any investment are not considered earned income.

The Corporate Plan

When you start to make real money, it may be advisable to consider changing to the corporate plan. Naturally, to do this you must convert your agency into a true corporation. The basic advantage is that you can now put away up to 25 percent of your salary and bonuses toward retirement, with a maximum limit (at present) of approximately $30,000 a year. The government increases this maximum every year to offset inflation, but even $30,000 a year is four times as much as the $7,500 the Keogh plan allows. Let's assume that at the age of 45 you've reached the point where you can put the maximum in a corporate plan every year and that this investment grows at the rate of 8 percent per year, compounded. At this rate, when you reach 60—15 years later—your equity in the plan would be $814,560. At 65, it would be $1,372,830. These are tidy sums to think about.

Your corporation can set aside an amount equal to 25 percent of your income, tax-deferred, through the use of two corporate plans. One is a profit-sharing plan that can equal a maximum of 15 percent of your income, and the second is a money-purchase pension plan where the corporation sets aside up to 10 percent of your income, tax-deferred. The pension plan is a definite commitment and whatever percentage is agreed upon at the instigation of the plan must be paid each year whether the company makes money or not.

Both plans must be approved by the IRS. The easiest way to accomplish this is to adopt plans the IRS has already approved. Many banks and insurance companies offer such master plans and, as a rule, you can easily adapt your needs to one of their plans. When you go this route, IRS approval is usually a mere formality.

If you can't find a suitable master plan, you can have a qualified attorney draw one up for you. You can expect to pay several thousand dollars, and it may take up to a year to gain IRS approval.

As with the Keogh plan, all employees must be included in your profit-sharing and pension plan.

If you choose a corporate plan that allows for self-direction of investments, you'll find a much more liberal set of conditions than with the Keogh plan. In choosing investments, you have the same options as with the Keogh plan. In addition, you can personally borrow funds from the plan for the purchase of a house or for a child's education, if the plan so provides.

As you can see, the more money you make, the more retirement benefits you can derive from your business. Planning for retirement is part of professional sales-agency management; if you start planning early enough, you'll be in good shape financially regardless of economic conditions at the time you decide to retire.

These are the highlights of the plans available to you under our current laws, summarized to make you aware of the excellent benefits that can accrue from planning ahead. When you embark upon your program, make certain you get good professional advice. Many conditions not mentioned in this brief review should be considered carefully before adopting a plan: employee rights, withdrawal schedules, and a host of others. A knowledgeable attorney, a banker, or a CPA would probably be the best sources for a fair appraisal of the retirement route you wish to take.

Sale of Your Business

If you begin early with a retirement program and plan well ahead for the sale of your business, your later years can be enjoyed without the financial concerns that face so many retirees today. Social Security benefits will probably never be sufficient to make you really comfortable, and most pensions received by corporate employees are fixed amounts that don't take into consideration the destructive effects of inflation.

On the other hand, if you've amassed a nest egg through a generous retirement plan, along with the sale of your business, the ravages of inflation can be offset through the wise investment of these funds. You can then have a worry-free retirement.

After reviewing the retirement benefits mentioned, you may decide you're not going to worry about selling your business, since you'll have sufficient retirement funds on hand at 65 to comfortably take care of your needs. And maybe you'll just want to keep working forever. Well, regardless of the attractive tables you've seen detailing how well-off you'll be in later years, it may not necessarily work out that way. Some of you will get a late start, and others may never make the big money necessary to fund a lucrative retirement program; you may approach later years in poorer financial shape than you'd like.

If you haven't planned well in advance for the profitable sale of your business, you may wake up some morning with no lines, very little savings, and a bleak future. Naturally, this doesn't happen overnight, but it can seem that way. It's always easier to put off decisions of this nature for another year, and as you get older you tend to dismiss the loss of an occasional line with one excuse or another. But even though there are successful reps who remain active into their seventies, principals tend to be attracted to agencies peopled by younger men and women. A successful older rep is the exception rather than the rule.

Of course, if your son or daughter is interested in carrying on the business, you will have an easier changeover. But even in that instance, good planning for the sale of the business to an heir can save estate taxes and prevent family squabbles in the event of your untimely death.

A good age to begin thinking about selling your business is your early fifties, and by the time you're 55 or 56 you should have a plan fairly well along.

Seldom can you make a straight cash sale to a total stranger or even a friend. Normally *you* are the agency, and the relationship between your principals and the agency is a personal one—not a salable item. However, by transferring this personal relationship to a buyer over a period of years, it's possible to make your agency a highly salable entity and realize a nice profit on it.

How is this done? Very carefully.

When you begin to transfer your relationship with your principals to a prospective buyer, you do so only after you have a binding agreement for the sale of your business. If you've brought a younger man to work as a direct salesman for your agency and you delegate much of the rep–principal communication to this person, you are already beginning to transfer your valuable relationship (essentially, your assets) with no guarantee that you'll receive anything for it. Remember, aside from a few desks and file cabinets, this is all you have to sell, so guard it closely.

Before selling your business, make sure you're negotiating with someone who is capable of running the agency profitably. After all, in 99 percent of the cases where businesses are sold, the purchase price is earned through profits the agency realizes in the five to ten years immediately following the sale. If the new owner is not a good businessman, you're not going to get your money.

To eliminate part of this danger, a typical sale calls for a ten-year payout, with control of the agency remaining in the hands of the seller for five or six years. Stock in the business is gradually transferred to the new owner, and he ultimately attains controlling interest. Hopefully, by that time the buyer will not only have learned the business but he will also be the driving force in the agency and have the complete trust of its principals.

How do you determine the worth of your agency? Most agencies are sold for a price that approximates two to three times the average annual gross commissions earned over the previous three or four years. In other words, if your agency has grossed an average of $100,000 per year for the past three or four years, your selling price should be somewhere between $200,000 and $300,000.

Of course, if you have an agency with several sales people, you'll be able to realize a lot more from the sale of your business than you would as a one-man agency, simply because you will have grossed larger commissions than Charlie Jones did working out of his house. In addition, you'll have a sales force that has been responsible for much of your success, and this group will represent the most logical buyer.

A good reference for your file is Melvin H. Daskal's reprint series titled "Valuation and Sale of Your Rep Business."* It is an excellent guide that will start you thinking about all the facets, including the tax consequences, of selling your business.

A good attorney, schooled in corporate law and a veteran of the ins and outs of the sale of a business, can be your biggest asset when you begin to think about selling out. So bring the right attorney in early, and the two of you can develop a plan that will allow for a profitable sale and an orderly transition.

Most reps probably don't really want to retire from active duty. Often the buyers of their businesses are happy to have them work one or two days a week, taking care of a few favorite customers and continuing to make a contribution to the success of the agency.

Another alternative is starting up a different type of business—one that may have always interested you. Provided you don't get foolish and invest your entire nest egg, this kind of challenge can bring renewed enthusiasm and sometimes result in considerable additional income.

Whatever your choices, plan early and enjoy.

* Available from MANA, $2.00. The author is MANA's CPA.

14
ALTERNATIVES
Other Routes to Your Own Sales Agency

THE METHODS USED to enter the agency business by the six successful reps who were described in the early chapters are by no means the only possible successful strategies. True, all six men followed certain basic principles: they began their agencies in home territories where they had previously established business relationships and every one of them sold products with which they were familiar. More importantly, they also were able, one way or another, to come up with funds that would carry them through until they could break even.

The lack of capital, and the question of how much is needed, probably stops more would-be reps than any other factor. Many of my acquaintances now working as direct salesmen would jump at the chance to become reps if only someone would eliminate the financial risk for them. This hesitation is what keeps the field rather sparse—new entries are scarce just when demand is increasing.

In addition to the techniques used by our six reps, there are some other methods that have helped would-be reps solve the problem of how to keep the wolf from the door during the early days. Although none of these can be used by all prospective reps because of differences in personality, background, and opportunity, it would be wise to keep them in the back of your mind in the event that your particular situation provides you with the opportunity to use some of the ideas mentioned here.

The Retainer Strategy

If a reputable company needs professional reps badly enough, it will consider using retainers. This means that the company will pay a monthly amount of $100 to $1,000 to a qualified newcomer in the field. The key, of course, is the word "qualified"; the company will not put its money on a novice unfamiliar with the rep way of conducting business or on someone who is obviously out of a job, nor will it back a person unfamiliar with the product line of the company. But if you have a good track record in your present job, have some familiarity with the agency business, and can persuade a prospective principal that you'll devote a lot of your time to its product, you may be able to get a sizable retainer for a stipulated period of time which will help you get started. If you can find two or more firms willing to part with a few hundred dollars a month, you will have what amounts to a maintenance income, although it does have a limited time span: you must produce within a given period or the funds will be stopped.

To take advantage of this short-term financing you have to search very aggressively. Put your intentions up front, but outline the reasons you feel you can contribute to the profitability of the principal. For instance, a direct man will cost the company about $3,000 a month. For a third of this you'll give the principal a large percentage of your time, plus the loyalty that is the natural result of being a retainer.

Naturally, it's not easy to find firms willing to part with a monthly amount. It goes against the very theory that most firms have when turning to reps—the theory that a rep costs them nothing until a sale is made.

This is, of course, fallacious thinking. Established reps are very selective about taking on new principals, because they risked a great deal to reach their present position of income and independence. Only occasionally will they take on a new line without some benefits up front, such as commissions on existing business.

Those reps just beginning their business are more likely to be targets of companies that feel reps should come free, mainly because they'll have difficulty finding established reps to take them on. This means that it will be hard for you as a new rep to find a principal that will invest retainer money in you, although the firms that are most likely to do so are those that have been using the rep method of selling for a good number of years. They are usually knowledgeable about the agency business and normally expect to hire established reps, but often they're not successful and therefore must turn to the newer people in the field. Therefore, watch "rep wanted" advertisements closely and, through use of the *Thomas Register* of American manufacturers and other directories, try to determine if the companies that are advertising have an established program of selling through reps.

One way to discover this status is to note where their sales offices are located. Many companies show this in the *Thomas Register*. By phoning one of the locations listed, you can find out if the sales office is company-owned or is run by a rep. If these offices are operated by reps, then you may have a prospective principal willing to consider a retainer if you can convince the sales manager of your qualifications.

Another—and perhaps more willing—source of retainer funds is foreign companies. I've visited with representatives of several foreign countries, mostly people belonging to trade associations who were seeking to help their members find out how to do business in this country. I found them mystified by our way of doing business and eager to learn how to attract reps for member companies of their associations.

The quickest way to find these companies is through local consulates. Most foreign governments have offices in our larger cities, and they usually have an executive on their staff who offers aid to firms in their country that want to do business in the United States. I've found them very eager to develop a listing of reps, since most American reps are not very interested in representing principals in foreign countries. This is a parochial attitude, because those who do represent good foreign firms often make attractive incomes.

You simply have to visit or write the consulates and make them aware of your interest in representing firms from their countries. You may as well declare your intentions at the same time. State that you will require a retainer and give them your fee range ($200–$500, or whatever you feel you can get on the basis of your qualifications). The consulate will file your application and advise you when they have a firm that can meet your terms. In many cases, executives of these companies will visit the U.S., and you will be able to sit down and visit with them personally, which will give you a better opportunity to find out what potential they offer.

Retainers are not easy to come by, but that doesn't mean you shouldn't make the effort if this is the only way you can obtain the funds necessary to supplement other sources of capital that you have available.

Company-Sponsored Agency

Another way to overcome the handicap of lack of start-up capital is through an agency financed by your present employer. There are two situations in which this route may be open to you.

1. A territory may be producing too little in revenue for your company. Because of the limited potential for your firm's profit there, it may never be able to justify keeping a direct man in place, so it may consider using a rep. But as we've discussed previously, many managements are reluctant to turn over existing business to an unknown rep, although they may look more kindly on the possibility of turning over this business to a salesman knowledgeable about the company and its products, and this is where you come in.

If you see a trend toward reps in certain areas, areas where you would like to locate, approach your sales manager and ask to be considered. Of course, a lot depends upon the commissions that the territory is producing from current customers. If you have little re-serve cash, $5,000 in commissions wouldn't go very far toward maintaining your solvency, but $20,000 would. And this is a lot less than the $40,000 it would take to keep a direct man in place. (Also, as an established rep with one line and an income, you'll find it much easier to obtain complementary lines.)

2. If you are an extremely successful direct salesman, one whom the company obviously wishes to keep happy, you may have excel-lent bargaining power. At your request the company may seriously consider making you a rep in one of their more successful territories and it may pay you commission on existing business. The territory could already be yours as a direct salesman, which would make things even easier for you.

In both of these examples, there is some danger because you've alerted the firm to the fact that you are eager to start your own agency. Before considering this course you should have a pretty good idea how your management will react. There are numerous cases of people who got into the rep business this way and who are now doing very well.

A Purchased Business

Here we have a roundabout way of beginning your own sales agency. It takes longer and can be risky, but my partner and I used it with excellent results.

Dave Braack and I had both worked for the same Chicago-based company for a number of years. It was a fine firm specializing in engineered products, and we were happy with our jobs. We worked closely with the company's reps and often envied their lifestyles and apparent financial successes. From time to time we daydreamed about entering the agency business.

In the late sixties, we witnessed a slow but steady deterioration in our company's ability to maintain a good profit level. Concerned by this trend, we began to think about possible alternatives. Our major emphasis, of course, was concentrated on the rep business.

One big stumbling block faced us, the same one that faces most prospective reps—we didn't have what we thought would be enough capital to last until breakeven day. Between us we could raise about $50,000 by selling our homes and other assets, but because we would be selling engineered products (which take a long time to sell), we knew the $50,000 wouldn't last long enough. Then we had a stroke of luck.

One of Dave's former classmates at college was an executive of a Chicago-based franchising firm that had a service franchise in Dallas. The firm confidently guaranteed that, with professional management, the Dallas franchise would reap handsome profits. The pro forma statement the Chicago company prepared looked like a direct path to the pot of gold at the end of the rainbow.

Having experienced midwestern winters most of our lives, Dave and I were excited by the prospect of moving to Dallas. We knew that beginning a rep business in an area where we had literally no business relationships would be much more difficult than starting our agency in Chicago, but the lure of a warmer climate and an expanding industrial complex in the Sunbelt made our decision easier—we would buy the franchise.

We had confided to Dave's friend that all we could raise was $50,000. The franchiser generously agreed that this would cover the down payment and allow a few thousand dollars for working capital. After suitable negotiations we signed an agreement calling for the down payment plus a note for an additional $70,000. In January 1969 we were off to Dallas.

Naturally, we hoped that our new company would make money, but we were willing to settle for a breakeven status that would permit us to launch our rep business on a modest income. Unfortunately, the service business we bought was in sad shape. Much of this was due to years of neglect along with poor operating results brought upon it by the burden of paying regular franchise fees back to the franchiser, as well as the necessity of purchasing supplies from the franchiser at noncompetitive prices. The franchise had no credit rating and a poor reputation in the Dallas area. We soon realized we had paid too much for it but we were committed; all we had was sunk into that business. Gradually we overcame our problems, and by the early part of 1973 we had moved into the profit column.

In the meantime we signed up principals and established customers in Texas and Oklahoma. At the franchise we had developed good managers, and so Dave and I split the duties of selling both in the franchise operation and in our rep business. The production end of the service business we left to others.

In May 1973—not quite five years later—the franchiser embarked upon a plan to buy back franchises in major marketing areas and run them as company-owned units. The plan eventually was financially disastrous, but fortunately the timing was right for us. We had just reached breakeven day at our sales agency and happily negotiated the sale of our business back to the franchiser.

Because we still owed a large debt and were in arrears on payments, we agreed to the elimination of the debt and cash payment to us of $25,000 for the assets of the business. We had orginally invested $50,000 in cash, and we received $25,000 for the business—thus the actual investment for establishing our sales agency amounted to $12,500 each—a real bargain. While I'm not recommending that you pull up stakes and leave your area of operations as we did, the purchase of a good, going business can be another route to establishing yourself in the rep field. It's also one way to get around the cardinal rule of having to start your agency in an area where you have established business relationships. Be careful, however, because there are several dangers in this approach.

- The business may take so much of your time you'll have none left for your agency.
- This plan is more suitable for a partnership arrangement since duties can be split and one partner can cover for the other. One man will find it difficult to run both businesses.
- You may buy a business that has no chance of succeeding and lose your investment.

It's essential that any business you buy be investigated thoroughly. Take your time and make sure it can turn a profit. Profitable businesses, unfortunately, are seldom for sale; when they are, they're expensive. If members of your family are willing to help out, you can put them to work in your purchased business, giving you more time to concentrate on the agency business. Another advantage is having a common office for your purchased business and your sales agency.

Beware of franchises. I can't make that point too strongly. Large, well-managed franchises, such as McDonald's, require hundreds of thousands of dollars to acquire; you have to be practically rich to own one. If you have this kind of money, all other things being equal, go right into the rep business; don't bother purchasing a going business.

Some smaller franchisers are often interested only in the "front" money you put up; they frequently lose interest in your well-being once they have your cash. Others are outright frauds, designed to separate the would-be entrepreneur from his money as quickly as possible. Even reputable franchisers may require up to 10 percent of a franchisee's gross sales as a continuing royalty for getting him started and for providing promotional and other services. Unfortunately, they frequently contribute little or nothing in the way of support to warrant your paying this continuing royalty. And 10 percent is often the franchisee's margin of profit, leaving him little after he has sent his monthly check to the franchising firm.

Yes, purchasing a going business is another alternative to the methods used by our six reps, but it entails a lot of risk. I've described this strategy mainly to show that the approaches to becoming a manufacturers' representative are limited only by your imagination and common sense.

Why Be a Manufacturers' Representative?

Many people in industry look longingly toward the day they can become a rep. Why this desire on the part of so many well-employed salesmen and others who enjoy good salaries and well-endowed fringe benefits? Why give up all those advantages to enter a business that is risky at best, frequently lonely, and requires herculean efforts to survive? Well, perhaps a strong entrepreneurial drive explains the motivation of most of them. But obviously there are some real advantages to owning your own agency. After ten years as a rep, here's what I like about my profession.

Independence. This is worth more than money, and is part of the American dream. Yes, in a sense you're still working for someone else and you must produce in order to retain your association with the companies you represent, but *how you work* is up to you. As an employed salesman, you have definite controls and continuing supervision. But as a rep, *you* decide when and where your calls will be made. If you linger an extra hour over lunch with an important customer—or with just a good friend—no eyebrows are raised when you return to the office. If you choose to work literally day and night one week and go fishing the next, you can. There is no need to request permission or sneak off without the boss's knowledge. *You* are the boss.

Of course, to enjoy your independence you must practice self-discipline. Independence doesn't mean less work and dedication; it simply means *you* choose when you work and how hard you work and whom you work for. I guess it can be summed up by the phrase *freedom of choice.*

Income. Those reps who make it to breakeven day usually prosper. That's why I've emphasized those early sacrifices—the end result is worth it. To sacrifice so that someday you can own your own hot dog stand may be fulfilling, if that's your goal, but it hardly ranks with the financial rewards that can be realized from a successful sales agency.

With the national average income for manufacturers' reps now reaching $50,000, the financial rewards of this business need no further explanation. In the corporate world, your $50,000 salary can disappear overnight as a result of a merger or a personality conflict. The rep business provides insurance against this type of loss through the rep's diversification of principals.

Still, even reps must be careful. One southwestern rep had a nice group of lines, but one of his principals started providing more and more income until he was making well over $100,000 from that line alone. He gradually lost his other lines as his other principals came to the conclusion that he was concentrating almost exclusively on his big producer. Because he became complacent about his major principal, he didn't bother to replace these lost lines. Then the bubble burst: Mr. Big Producer changed managements and terminated the rep in favor of a direct-employee salesman. He is now back working as a direct salesman himself for a modest salary.

My strongest warning: keep those eggs in several baskets so that you can survive the loss of a line or two.

Self-satisfaction. There's simply no substitute for the satisfying feeling of starting your own business from scratch and succeeding. It's so gratifying, in fact, that many successful small businessmen are almost obnoxious about it. Income, of course, is important, but to enjoy what you're doing every day is actually more important. Lack of job satisfaction is one of the major problems in industry today, but it should never be one of yours. You'll have problems in your business, of course, but overall you'll be setting out each day with the actual possibility that something really big might happen: a big order, a fine new principal, and many other potentials that the self-employed manufacturers' representative can look forward to.

You're in a growing business. It's true that small businesses are being sold off to large conglomerates with their own direct-employee sales people. But I find these conglomerates have the same sales-cost problems other firms have. Consequently, their new acquisitions are usually encouraged not only to continue with their rep forces but, in many cases, to change from direct men to reps.

Keep in mind that many new companies are forming every year, and the only practical way for them to market their goods is through manufacturers' representatives. So the need for good professional reps is increasing daily.

You can be part of this elite group of independent salesmen. If you build your business on solid effort and conscientious dedication to serving your customers and principals with a high degree of professionalism, you'll spend the rest of your career in a productive and enjoyable adventure.

INDEX